REDEFINING ROLES AND RELATIONSHIPS

Our Society in the New Millennium

Papers from the Third Rural Resource Development Conference

Edited by Harry Bohan and Gerard Kennedy

VERITAS

Published 2001 by
Veritas Publications
7/8 Lower Abbey Street
Dublin 1

ISBN 1 85390 562 3

British Library Cataloguing
in Publication Data.
A catalogue record for
this book is available
from the British Library.

Cover by Avid Design, Limerick
Printed in the Republic of Ireland by Betaprint Ltd, Dublin

Veritas books are printed on paper made from the wood pulp of
managed forests. For every tree felled, at least one tree is planted,
thereby renewing natural resources.

Fr Harry Bohan and his team chose a conference title that touched on a subject that was in danger of being subsumed by an ever-changing society.

The 'Redefining Roles and Relationships' conference has facilitated a meeting of minds, a meeting of concepts and ideas. I am in no doubt that many issues will be more effectively addressed as a result of the commitment of those who attended and participated in this conference.

Barney Whelan
Manager, ESB Public Relations
Conference Sponsor

CONTENTS

DAY TWO

PART ONE: ECONOMICS, AS IF PEOPLE MATTERED?

PART TWO: CAN ANYTHING BE PERMANENT IN A CHANGING WORLD?

FOREWORD

Harry Bohan

I think there are good reasons for suggesting that the modern age has ended. Today, many things indicate that we are going through a transitional period when it seems that something is on the way out and something else is painfully being born. It is as if something were crumbling, decaying and exhausting itself, while something else, still indistinct, were arising from the rubble.

Václav Havel,
President, Czech Republic

This is a special and indeed unique time in Irish history. As an island we are at the beginning of peace and can fully celebrate our rich cultural diversity. We are experiencing extraordinary change. Technology has altered the nature of Irish society. The communications industry and culture are seen as the embodiment of progress. From being a static stable society, Ireland has suddenly become part of the globalised world.

Coinciding with these new beginnings is the sense amongst ordinary people that the institutions on which they depend are failing them. The bonds between individuals and these institutions have loosened and even broken. In a short space of time Irish society has moved from one in which people's lives were largely organised for them to a society in which people are forced to be in charge of their own destiny. To a large extent, they are called on to write their own script for life instead of acting out a part someone else has written for them. And yet, as a people, we are heavily influenced by global forces.

There is a need to understand how systems and institutions are responding to people's needs, to understand change and to equip people at a personal level so that they can effect change at an organisational level. Our third annual conference, 'Redefining Roles and Relationships', was an attempt to respond to this need.

The papers presented at the conference are contained in this book. I hope they capture for you, the reader, some of what this conference was about. The papers attempt to address these questions:

- How do we handle the next ten years?
- What values shape modern society?
- Putting people at the centre of things!
- Can anything be permanent in a changing world?

The current situation of prosperity seems to exist side by side with disconnectedness from self, others, creation, Creator. The first thing that we must do, and that our conference attempted to do, is to recognise that a problem exists. Proposing solutions then calls for leadership at all levels of society. To that end, individuals were called on as they left the conference to examine what they could do within their own circle of influence to respond to the ideas, ideals and vision brought to them during the conference.

The future calls for reintegration of contemplation with action. As promoters of the conference, we recognise the value of these events and the collective conversation and reflection. We are also committed to action that will address the questions raised. As a society we must embrace the radical, invest in society and rescue the deep values that made and make Ireland unique. Our aim is to establish an institute that will have international significance. It will bring together global scholars to consider universal themes, redressing the balance from functionality to imagination; from productivity to creativity; from careless to caring. Through this institute, researchers will seek to find a counterbalance to consumerism and to optimise the manner in which Ireland encounters the intersection of the global with the local. Individuals and groups from all walks of life will be encouraged to gather and reflect on life lived from deep values: sensitivity to the sacred; rekindling memory. Already we have a network of corporate executives considering the restoration of balance between work and lifestyle and plans are well advanced for a research study of the family. We pledge to you our commitment to this initiative and ask for your continued support. By our next conference we intend having a fully developed plan to share with you. I look forward to seeing you there.

We are grateful to a number of people for making this third annual conference such a success. The staff of Rural Resource Development Ltd, the conference committee, and the volunteers who gave so generously of their time made a big contribution. They were ably co-ordinated by Máire Johnston. Mary Clancy-Rice spent months prior to the conference contacting corporations and individuals. The fact that over 600 people attended the whole conference and approximately 1,000 touched in to some part of it, indicates the excellent organisation that went into it. However, people would not have shown interest if it were not for the quality of the speakers and the topics. We want to thank the speakers for their excellent presentations and thorough preparation, and Mick O'Connell for the official opening. Our chairpeople had the most difficult job of all and we are grateful to both Kate and David. To everyone who attended as delegates, we say thanks. We want to thank the West County Hotel, and our main sponsors, the ESB. We are also grateful for the considerable media coverage of the event, especially in the lead-up to the conference.

Preparations for Conference 2001 are already well underway, as indeed are several other outcomes from the conferences.

OPENING NIGHT

Conference Introduction
Harry Bohan

Opening Address: 'My Time and Place'
Mick O'Connell

Conference Introduction

Harry Bohan

I want to briefly outline why we are organising these conferences, what is happening in between, what is proposed to happen and what this year's conference is all about. We are trying to read the signs of our times; we are trying to understand change and its implications for people 'where they are'. We are doing this because we believe that if we don't at least try to understand change, a lot of what we value could disappear and fundamental connections could be broken.

Things have been changing since the beginning of time but extraordinary transformations have been taking place in the last few years. We are aware of great progress but uneasy about what is happening to us as a people. Trying to understand this change seems to be important in order to restore balance. Maybe some of the changes that are taking place are so obvious that they don't get noticed and so there is a need to identify and articulate them.

Since the mid 1990s we have been very successful in building an economy. We have one of the most impressively performing economies in the world. Ireland will soon be one of the wealthier member states of the EU. Its economy provides work for everybody born here and indeed for many who were not born here. Massive resources are being invested, designed to ensure that the volume of economic activity will continue. It was initiated by a broad range of actors and is now driven by the private sector – corporations and developers.

Coinciding with the strong performance of the Irish economy, however, is a wide and deep concern that all is not well. There is an acute sense that these achievements are coming at a very high price. It is often expressed as a concern for what constitutes quality of life issues – family life, neighbours, place. The impressions of dis-ease in contemporary Ireland are now being buttressed by quantitative indicators in such areas as marriage breakdown, stress in the workplace, suicide rates and levels of substance abuse. Personal experiences of loneliness and depression bring home the message that we might be becoming slaves of technology – of the machine – and disconnecting from one another. We are aware that modern communications technology is producing the jobs and through it we can easily connect to the wider world, but we wonder how we are communicating with one another. There are signs too that institutions and structures can become devalued and indeed irrelevant very quickly these days. These are often the institutions that are dealing with values and quality of life issues.

There are clear indications that many government and public services are finding it difficult to cope with change – medical services, education/schooling, public housing/planning, and also the Church. It is clear now that those of us – clerics and lay people – formed to maintain the institution now have problems responding to the spiritual needs of people. I would like to quote from an article by Donagh O'Shea, a Dominican, on the theme 'Formation in the post-modern age': *It seems incredible now that spirituality was a Cinderella subject in seminaries. The real stuff was canon law and 'practical morals'. You could build houses with that stuff – or sections of skyscrapers. When theology doesn't grow directly out of spiritual experience it carries no credibility.*

It is a good sign that some people within the Church have such insight and can now clearly identify the importance of spiritual experience through meditation and the importance of discipleship of Him who said *'I am the Way.'*

This concern is not based on nostalgia or motivated by any attempt to 'talk up' the quality of life that individuals, families and communities enjoyed at a time when we were not so well off. Nor is it a mistrust of prosperity and affluence. It is characterised more by a concern that national economic success and a more business-oriented culture should be treated as the opportunity for a genuine expression of human opportunities. When we were poor we were connected because we needed one another. It can be more difficult to handle prosperity than it is to handle poverty when almost everyone is poor.

I am suggesting that the connections (social capital) that have so enriched and enlivened Irish cultural and individual life have been underpinned and sustained by an openness to intimacy. As this fabric becomes loosened and the ties of connectedness to place, to others, to past or to God all become weakened, the individual is cast adrift and has nothing to draw upon for emotional or social nurturing.

GNP is how we measure the health of our economy, but GNP doesn't measure our individual, family or community life, nor our compassion or devotion to civic and social life. In short, it measures everything except that which makes life worthwhile. In the areas of life where people find meaning there would seem to be a void.

In a country that was for so long dominated by institutions, we have come to think of ourselves as belonging not to a country but to an economy, in which the worlds of work and amusement are at the centre of life. And so, if we are forgetting something, if we must work towards balance, there is a need to redefine the role of institutions and to identify how we might redevelop relationships at a time when we are fostering the cult of the individual. There is a need too to foster more personal social responsibility and less government.

In 1998 we ran our first conference, titled 'Are We Forgetting Something?' We were delighted with the inputs and the response from a cross-section of Irish society. Our second conference, in 1999, 'Working Towards Balance', was even better. Our aim was to create debate about some of the very fundamental issues that are affecting us. It is clear now that the idea of reflecting together on what direction we are taking is healthy. We had come to over-rely on the media for this. As the debate and reflection has evolved, it is becoming clearer that, yes, we are forgetting some things that we need to address as a matter of urgency. Some of these are:

- The changes that we – our generation – are now experiencing in Ireland and being called on to cope with, took place over three or four generations in other societies;
- We need to acknowledge that by far the most important requirement for building an economy, not to mention building a society, is people. Without people who are prepared to work, there will be no corporation, no commerce. From where do these people come? They come from ordinary society, more specifically from families.

- What is happening to family? The traditional model of family, often referred to as the 'Kellogg Family' following the happy family illustrations on the cornflakes boxes, is now just one model among many. The variations of family life are endless.
- Our present economic growth rate, welcome and all as it is, is beginning to go out of control. Tigers can devour us, especially when they run wild and uncontrolled. We continue to invest in our economy, but we cannot house our own population, not to mention those coming in. We are failing to solve our poverty problem and in fact the gap between the 'haves' and 'have-nots' has widened to the extent that we are now the second worst in Europe. And there is no greater poverty than that which sits beside great wealth.

Some of the speakers at these conferences underlined the radical choices that are now open to individuals and families as a result of rapid economic and technological change and the need to develop a 'philosophy of enough' in a society of growing but unequally distributed wealth.

We can all easily blind ourselves to the fact that institutions and structures can change and disappear very quickly. In a few short years, towards the end of the '80s, the entire communist political system that had grown up over half a century virtually disappeared. Almost none of the commentators foresaw this astonishing development. There were enough subtle movements to make it so obvious that this was going to happen that it was never noticed.

There are real signs that this is happening today – to religious, political and business institutions and organisations. When trust is broken it is not easily reclaimed. It certainly has to be earned, and that only happens by reference to the people for whom these institutions and organisations exist. They have no meaning without reference to the people.

For example, since its dawning in the 1760s in the Western world and in the 1960s in Ireland, the industrial revolution has been challenging morals, ethics and values. The communications revolution of the '90s has certainly challenged them. The structures through which many of these operate are often unable to respond to the needs of people in the face of these great changes. The language and symbols they use do not relate to contemporary society. The result is that these institutions and organisations get bypassed by the masses who are shaped by global influences.

Our conferences to date are also highlighting the serious pressure that other supports that connected us with one another in the past, such as the family and community, are coming under. There is a picture emerging of a society that was once held together by the family and community now becoming a society of disconnected individuals. The principal causes are time pressure, because people are so busy, and the mobility in jobs and residence, imposed by the way the economy is organised. Yesterday, a secondary-school teacher told me that 70 per cent of senior students go home every day to nobody. There is an exaggerated independence fostered by the consumer culture and above all by television and the general impact of electronic technology on the way we relate to one another. Richard Putman's pithy summary is sobering: 'People now watch *Friends* instead of having them.'

Note the number of people who will now travel to a football match on their own. A big percentage of people who watch television watch it on their own. We are a sports-loving nation and yet we play sports less often or not at all. Fewer of us are involved in community and civic action and fewer of us vote.

These are some of the issues that have been highlighted at our conferences to date. We now want to suggest or indeed challenge institutions, corporations and organisations to think about redefining their roles and values in the face of these extraordinary changes and how they can support and facilitate the two vital systems of family and community. We believe that the reflection and debate that has taken place in these conferences so far has been useful and some steps have been taken to fill the obvious void that is there. We believe too in the importance of developing partnerships between the corporate world, the community, government bodies and churches.

The corporate world has become one of the great shapers of society and has become so central to life in Ireland that we felt it important to set up a small network of people from that world. From an early stage it became clear that there is increasing pressure on businesses to address the needs of all its stakeholders, especially those who come from ordinary society, and more specifically from family and community. A tight labour market is demanding greater work/life balance. Employees want to work in a business culture that aligns with their personal values and supports them, so that they feel they are able to bring their whole self to work, without seriously neglecting their family or community relationships. Irish society has just moved from an adherence to institutions that imposed their will on the people. We have to be convinced that the rapid erosion of one type of structure heretofore held largely unaccountable will not simply be replaced by others. People all over the world are now unhappy with the unaccountable power of corporations, as evidenced by demonstrations at the recent World Trade Organisation meeting in Seattle.

So in order to ensure that the volume of economic activity continues, and that we continue to support and facilitate individuals, families and communities, business organisations have to come up with better ways of operating. In effect, a new business model needs to evolve – just as other institutions and organisations have to now search for new beginnings.

Government and community leaders are demanding greater involvement of business in the social fabric of society and so the whole concept of trying to restore the balance must be done in partnership between business, government, community, education and religious leaders.

We must be clear that, as pointed out to us in last year's conference, *'We have no history to guide us on how to handle the next ten years.'* We don't even have a language for it and so, unlike the way institutions operated in the past, we must begin the process of searching rather than compliance, and we must continue to remind ourselves that this search has no meaning apart from human beings, their relationships and where they are. In the past two years, we have been involved in this process through the establishment of an Applied Research Centre and the identification of key issues such as the state of the family in Ireland, balance between work and lifestyles, where our values are coming from, participation in civic and community life, settlements and spatial planning.

The reflection and research in all these issues is being carried out with strong participative dimensions, through focus groups, corporate networks, community and professional groups in order to create a movement that will highlight the value of these issues in society. We are now proposing to take this much further by setting up an international institute that will have the exclusive concern of ensuring that the critical issues that give meaning to life will receive the attention, resources and support that the world of commerce is receiving.

So, in summary, our aim is to facilitate reflection and debate on issues that are critical for meaningful living. We are following this up with action that will help us to work together in the reconstruction of society. We will be arguing that connectedness has been at the core of our identity as a people but also of our achievements as a people.

A conference like this attempts to explore the elements of society that are contributing to the process of cultural disintegration, and, crucially, it attempts to identify remedial actions that can reverse some of these patterns.

In conclusion, the following is a message to the conference from Mary Robinson, United Nations High Commissioner for Human Rights:

> I am happy to send good wishes to the Chairman, Fr Harry Bohan, and all those involved in the Ennis conference organised by Rural Resource Development. I regret that my commitments do not permit me to be with you in person, though to judge from what I hear about the recent weather in Ireland it might have been difficult for me to get there!
>
> The reports I am receiving suggest that these annual conferences in Ennis are establishing themselves as an important date in the calendar and meeting a need for serious discussion about major social and ethical issues of the day. In the area of human rights I find that open debate about issues is the beginning of understanding and, hopefully, of strengthening the culture of respect for the human rights of all. One of the most welcome features of modern Ireland is the willingness to have such debate and to confront even the complex, sensitive subjects that in the past would have been avoided.
>
> Ireland is enjoying a welcome period of economic growth, which is bringing prosperity on a level that past generations

could only dream of. Yet we know that wealth does not solve all problems and indeed brings along with it new responsibilities and challenges. Ensuring that everyone gets to share in our national properity and that those who come to our shores are treated with dignity and fairness are obvious examples. So, too, are the themes you will address at the conference relating to the personal goals that people would like to set for themselves and how they wish to relate to one another.

I am sure that this will be stimulating, enjoyable conference and I wish you well in your discussions.

Opening Address: 'My Time and Place'

Mick O'Connell

I was born on Valentia Island in 1937. It was only by a slight quirk of fate that I was born there. Our ancestral home for generations had been Begnis Island, a mile to the north, but in 1933 my father and mother, with their three children, decided to uproot and cross the channel. They bought a small holding and settled on Valentia. I arrived there a few years later. Years afterwards I asked my father why he'd moved and he said to me that it was purely for pragmatic reasons. He was a very successful fisherman and later a life-boat man. He said that trying to cater for a young family and to be involved in the fishing industry at the same time was impossible.

Valentia Island in the 1930s was a very advanced place in comparison to other places on the mainland, and other islands in particular. There was a population of 1,100. We had three national schools, two doctors, a village hospital, a creamery and all sorts of services. We had a garda barracks, with a sergeant and four gardaí, post offices, two Roman Catholic churches and one Church of Ireland, with priests and parson. We had a train service to the ferry point across the way. But what made the place particularly important was the presence of many outsiders. Valentia Radio had a station that was based on Reendrolan Point. The Commissioners of Irish Lights had their headquarters there for the life-boats serving the Skellig's lighthouses. Then there was the headquarters of the Western Union Cable Company, where many people worked. Some came from the south of England. They came from all over Ireland to work on the lighthouses and so on. At the time it was very unusual to have such a great mix of people. Those people who came added greatly to the economic and cultural life of the island. Then there were cable ships of all sorts and Spanish, French and Welsh trawlers used to visit. As a young lad growing up there, I saw registrations from Newfoundland, Nova Scotia, Denmark, La Rochelle, Milford Haven, and trawlermen from all those places. I saw that the level of poverty of some of those visitors was a lot higher than that of the people of Valentia. These days we hear a lot about asylum seekers and refugees. In my time I remember a boat from the Baltic Sea with Latvians on board. They berthed in Valentia. They lived on board the vessel and moved off again.

As regards employment on the island, the majority were smallholders, with a few strong farmers, and some fishermen. Generally it was a time when things were not easy on either land or sea. The only reward was to be reaped by honest toil. There was no other way.

My national school at the time was a mixed school. All the children of the parish went there, both Catholic and Protestant. After lunch was catechism time and I noticed that a few Protestant lads, with names like Longland, Milesoupe and so on, had to absent themselves. I found it very strange that they had to be away from the class; it was a kind of segregation from the start. We see it in Northern Ireland; it happened in Valentia too. 'Who made the world?' etc. – I thought these kinds of questions were just as applicable to the Protestants.

After finishing national school only about half the children would go forward to second-level education. The other half would go home and stay there for a few years. Some would get jobs and a lot of them would emigrate. I see that as a big contrast to now. The door is open for second-level education to all now. Those of us who went to secondary school went across to the mainland by boat and cycled to Cahirciveen School. After a number of years the vast majority would finish at that and try to find work. My father was persuaded to ask me to go to college and I went to University College, Cork, for a year. I felt rather uneasy as there was no family history of an academic background and I couldn't see where it was leading. My father supported me there. In those days a man of eighteen or nineteen years was supposed to be self-sufficient, so when I got the opportunity to work with the Western Union Cable company back on the island I jumped at it. In those times I couldn't see anything beyond going to college. Today a lot of people go on to third-level education, and I can identify with the ones who haven't come from an academic background. If that isn't there, it can be very difficult.

It was back on the island that I made a breakthrough on the sporting scene. I had always played Gaelic football with the young fellows on the island. Then I got my place on the Kerry senior team. For the next few years of my young manhood, all my spare time was spent playing football with the county team and with local teams. In those days sport was purely recreational. I played it in my spare time and did my job. I remember I would come back from Croke Park after playing on a Sunday, travel home in the middle of the night, and then make sure I would be back for work the next morning. There was a clear division – work was work and play was play.

Coming from a place like Valentia where you hadn't many facilities, you had to improvise. A lot of adjustments to your life had to be made in order to be involved. In a way, that made it more exciting for me. If something comes too easy to a person there is less satisfaction. In my case, I saw it as a hurdle to be overcome, and I found it pretty satisfying and fulfilling. I played under the flag of the Gaelic Athletic Association for a great number of years. I am not involved in the officialdom of the organisation but I must give them great credit for what they have done. The organisation is a model as an amateur organisation, providing facilities for young people from all over Ireland. I hope it does not lose its soul with the advent of all these new demands. Some of the members who are availing of GAA facilities are becoming more and more demanding. I think that the amateur ethos is the best one for the young men and women involved today. No doubt excellence can only be aspired to through professionalism, but a person can get great personal satisfaction from being involved as an amateur. In my particular case this was something – being involved, overcoming great difficulties – that I was glad to have the opportunity to do. I often wonder about sports today. I think we can see on a worldwide basis, in the Olympic games, for example, that there is something not very pure about it. I think that is a great pity, as I believe that young people need a different outlook on sport. It is not right to get the advantage over anyone or out of sport by foul means, whether that is by taking drugs or by any other means. In my time it was pure amateur and that made it very fulfilling.

I later delved into politics. I became a member of Kerry County Council as an independent. That means many things to many people, but I would like to explain what it meant to me. It meant that I would not ally with any political party. I always believed that any citizen should have the right to stand for local government. I think that the more local the government is, the more people will be interested in it. County Councils in general are portrayed as a bit of a joke, as having no relevance to people in their ordinary lives, but I can say from firsthand experience of my time in the County Council that they have great relevance to people in their ordinary lives. Roads, water, sewage, planning, fire fighting, waste disposal – all these are handled by the County Council and I took a great interest in these matters. I think my time there gave me a great insight into what it is to try to help people.

What I tried to do in the County Council was to give people a chance to empower themselves. I had several motions to try to get people to be independent and to fight for their rights and get them. Others in political parties very often disagreed with this approach. In Ireland the clinic system seems to operate. That means that people in all political ranks, from Dáil Éireann down, run clinics. I felt it would be better if that were left to the civil servants. The politicians themselves should be involved with policies. In the County Council I was trying to have people's rights available to them without resorting to these clinics, to ministers, and so on. On public matters generally I think that a lot of people do not like to get involved too much because they see it as a bit of a racket. My response to that is that the future of our children is in the hands of the politicians. Politics and sports are as clean or dirty as they are practised. I think one of the things that stops people from becoming involved in politics is the way that it is practised. The system of clinics does not give the opportunity for people to be independent. Many better systems are often suggested but are immediately shot down. I cannot understand why there is no progressive means to improve local government in this country.

One of the changes that I have noticed in society is how affluent people have become in my lifetime. There is a lot of talk about poverty in Ireland. I don't believe the figures that say that one-third of the people are impoverished in this country. It's all relative of course. I believe we never had it so good. There are great opportunities in educational matters, in health, and in housing. What was a luxury in the past has become a necessity today, and people are still not satisfied.

I used to draw the old-age pension for my uncle in the 1940s. It was 7/6d a week. Nowadays I am told that it is £96. In those days he could get thirteen loaves of bread for his allowance. Today you would get over one hundred loaves of bread for the £96. In spite of our present affluence, happiness and contentment seem to be missing.

There is another aspect of life that I have observed and that is emigration. All the counties of the West of Ireland have suffered from this. Emigration was compulsory, not like nowadays. In bygone days I met men who had to work abroad and indeed I worked abroad with them myself. They came home for short breaks to their families. That was a very sad thing altogether. Thank God that day has passed.

Down the ages there have been some awful hardships and levels of poverty in Ireland, but at present I cannot understand the levels of complaining. Since third- and second-level grant-aided education came in, it is often the ones who benefit most from it that are at the forefront of campaigns with pressure groups and sectional interests, getting extra benefits for themselves. I would have thought that those educated people would be aware that they have had it much better than their forebears. They should be tolerant and not make demands on the finances of the country. I think that the well-being of your fellow citizens is the most basic concern a person can have. The sectional interests that people in this country have is appalling. I am aghast at a 30 per cent pay claim by people in permanent pensionable jobs. No one seems to have the courage to speak out and tell the truth. These types of conferences are the kind of independent voice that we need to speak out on such issues.

Valentia Island is still a beautiful place, but it has changed. The population is now down to six hundred and has stabilised at that. The movement from the rural areas in these parts started many years ago. The Blasket Islands, the lighthouses and Begnis Island are totally abandoned now. In Valentia we do not have a sergeant or a garda. The post office is closed. The doctors are gone, probably due to a centralisation policy among themselves. We still have a village hospital, which means that the elderly of the island can now spend the last of their time on the island. It is an example of what is local and small and it can be held up as a model of what can be achieved locally. We are very lucky to still have it.

I really regret the loss of our first-class public transport system. There is no local transport system to replace it. In many parts of Ireland, particularly the West, the same thing has happened. I understand that railway lines cannot be financed to the same degree as in the past, but subsidised public transport can be justified to give people the choice of where they want to live. There is a trend, not only in Ireland but worldwide, for people to leave the rural areas and move into town and cities. We all know that the vast majority of crime, drug abuse and criminal activity is concentrated in the big centres of population. In my young days, anyone who wanted to travel had access to public transport. Today people in rural areas have been let down very badly in that way. We get a lot of lip-service about decentralisation, but there is tokenism attached to it. There is one department going to Nenagh and another going to Castlebar. There is one going to Cavan and now I know of another going to my own area – the Minister for Justice and Law Reform is bringing one to Cahirciveen. It sounds great, but I would much prefer if there was a good transport system. Proper decentralisation means that whether it is Clare, Kerry, Offaly or Donegal, the services should be on a par with the big centres of population. A basic transport system, post offices, and so on, are important to any young person growing up. If they see that their own place is not worthy of these services, then that place is bound to be diminished in their minds.

I am very lucky myself. I am the only one of a family of nine to be back on the island. The trend of families leaving the islands is very strong. Sometimes there are entire families who leave. It is a beautiful place to live. I have been very fortunate to be there with my wife Rosaleen and my family. That sense of locality, that sense of roots – I think that's something that is being diminished in Ireland now, and I don't know if it can be changed. I got a long letter from a man who I knew as a young boy. He was a fine footballer on the island. He is now a doctor, living in Dublin. He spent all his young life in Kenya. He wrote his first long letter to me last year. He was full of nostalgia for the old days and he was asking and reminiscing about old times. It brought home to me how fortunate I was and all those who can live where their roots are.

Living on an island, people often say to me 'you are very remote'. I say to them 'remote from where?' The cities are very remote from the rural. I am very lucky to be back on Valentia. It is a difficult place to live and to make a living, but there are compensations. It is true that if someone had special interests they may have to forgo them, but the advantages outweigh the disadvantages. For example, I can still go up Carrantuohill; walk the beach; go for a trip with my son Diarmuid in the boat around the island. That is something money couldn't buy. In the city I wouldn't have anything like that and to me that is most important. I think that the best things in life are free. I am delighted to enjoy and have all that I have.

I suppose the last O'Connell to be here in Ennis was Daniel, long ago. We come from the same part of the country and Daniel was a man who in his time was criticised left, right and centre. He was blamed for not supporting the language, which I think is a pity, but I suppose he saw that people who were in abject poverty could improve themselves by learning a little English. I don't know if he was good or bad, but I was mistaken for him once. I am sure I will never be immortalised to his extent. A Killarney taxi driver was driving some American tourists around Cahirciveen. They said that they would like to visit O'Connell's place. The driver, who had never studied history but enjoyed football, said 'He is over there in the street now' (he had just passed me). The American said, 'What are you talking about?' and the driver said, 'Oh yes, I will bring him over to you now'. 'The man I am talking about died in 1847,' said the American. 'Oh, that's the other fellow', said the driver.

I wish the conference every success. *Go raibh míle maith agaibh go léir.*

Day One

Part One: How do we handle the next ten years?

Contemplating Alternative Relationships of Power
in a Historical Perspective
Gearóid Ó Tuathaigh

Rebuilding Social Capital:
Restoring the Ethic of Care in Irish Society
Maureen Gaffney

Part Two: What Values Shape Modern Society?

Rise of Science, Rise of Atheism: Challenge to Christianity
Bill Collins

Social Justice and Equality in Ireland
Kathleen Lynch

View From the Chair
Kate Ó Dubhchair

Contemplating Alternative
Relationships of Power

Gearóid Ó Tuathaigh

Many of the recent critiques of the contemporary values and the future direction of Irish society, while in no sense denying the reality and the real benefits accruing from the recent phase of economic growth and wealth creation, have featured a number of recurring, key concerns. Powerlessness or, rather more provocatively, disempowerment is a predicament regularly ascribed to (or claimed by) individuals and groups who complain of disadvantage or victimisation on the basis of social class, or gender, or geographical location, or, increasingly, colour or ethnic origin. The feeling of being powerless to effect improvement or change in one's situation is a condition with which large numbers of people – whole communities or segments of society – increasingly seem or frequently claim to be afflicted, when faced with the impersonal forces of global economics, or the incremental disintegration of their local community through demographic anaemia and its consequential institutional impoverishment (e.g., the closure of a garda barracks, bank, school, church).

Or again, it is utterly routine nowadays to encounter a curious emotional cocktail of anger, bewilderment and fatalistic resignation among one's acquaintances and among members of the general public in Ireland in the face of massive evidence of systemic venality – institutional and personal – among sections of the elite in Ireland; of widespread bureaucratic incompetence and indifference to public inconvenience and pain; of dark swathes of social deprivation, poverty and suffering in the midst of a society generating and consuming wealth at an unprecedented level. What for some analysts are merely the paradoxes of a growth economy in a liberalised economic regime, seem to many others to be the repulsive downside of a greedy society functioning increasingly in a moral vacuum.

But the abiding message from public discussion of these issues – casually or in public debate in the various media – is one of powerlessness, the concluding refrain of many discussions being 'It's terrible, I know, but what can you do about it?' This sense of powerlessness – of not being able to creatively engage the structures of power through which 'the condition of things' is determined or changed – demands careful consideration.

Of course, this condition is not unique to Ireland or the Irish; one has ample evidence of similar feelings of powerlessness being articulated widely in many other developed, 'open', democratic societies in our contemporary world. The seemingly inexorable, integrating forces of globalisation, under western liberal-capitalist auspices, undoubtedly constitute a common source of this widespread feeling of resignation or powerlessness in communities, whether they be in inner-city Dublin or Detroit or Doonbeg.[1]

But it may be argued that there are particular aspects of Ireland's historical experience that exacerbate or deepen this almost fatalistic attitude towards a state of affairs with which large numbers of people are unhappy, indeed, indignant, but which they do not believe it to be in their competence to change. Even some of the activists – community leaders, advocates of various versions of a 'counter-culture' – who are striving to counter this syndrome of popular passivity or resignation, have difficulty finding a language or an effective strategy for mobilising popular anxiety or discontent towards purposeful ends.

Part of the reason for this relative failure to date may rest with an inadequate sensitivity on our part to the historical context in which attitudes towards power, institutions, development and happiness ('the good life') have been shaped in contemporary Ireland. The purpose of this paper is to contribute to this necessary task of historical sensitisation. Hopefully, the outcome of this enquiry will not only be a sharper sense of the historical context for our current predicament, but also some pointers, at least, towards identifying where we might make a start in taking actions that have some prospect of allowing us to shape rather than simply to await our future. I am mindful of the fact that historians have no claim to public attention outside of their competence to offer some insights into and interpretations of *past* events: they would do well to steer clear of the vatic or the prophetic in their commentaries. But I am also aware that Fr Harry Bohan prefers (perhaps insists would be more appropriate) that any analysis of our past or current predicament should have some forward-looking dimension to it and, if not robustly prescriptive, that it should at least suggest some ways of reading the map, with its alternative routes, for the road immediately ahead. Accordingly, in this essay I will seek to offer an historical context from which we might contemplate alternative relationships of power, and take a modest look forward to what we might usefully do in order to advance from where we are now.

The first or primary issue with which we are basically concerned, therefore, is the feeling of powerlessness that many people are experiencing in the face of the logic of globalisation: a feeling of remoteness (spatially and vertically, in the power ladder), and even of powerlessness or inadequacy in their capacity to grasp fully the complexity of the logic of globalisation (the forces of the 'free market' – economic, financial, cultural). More locally in Ireland, there is also the feeling of powerlessness in the face of the more scandalous (i.e., giving scandal on moral and ethical grounds) aspects of institutional life in Ireland itself, where major political, business and religious institutions all seem guilty, on the evidence to date, of serious betrayal of trust – and, as it appears, of other more specifically criminal wrong-doing.

Secondly – and in certain respects connected with this sense of powerlessness in the face of decisions taken elsewhere by others or in respect of wrong-doing and betrayal by seemingly unaccountable members of key élite institutions within our society – there is the issue of the diminishing role of community in advanced societies in our time. To put it another way, there is a growing sense of isolation and atomisation being felt by large numbers of people (clearly a source of anxiety, concern and distress to them) in the more advanced industrial or post-industrial societies, as sociability is affected by technology, by mobility, by urban living in a highly individualised culture of achievement and consumption, with the privatisation of pleasure or self-gratification (lives lived in home-alone flatland or through house-bound TV viewing, the 'walkman', and internet down-loading), with a work culture based on high specialisation and individualist task-allocation; with even routine domains of sociability threatened with eclipse by advancing technology (ATMs in place of face-to-face bank transactions, computer shopping and e-living creating the possibility of further 'insulation' against direct human contact). The rituals and habits of social bonding have been weakening in the face of these 'cultural' changes in economically/technologically advanced societies (pre-eminently the US), and, as Dr Maureen Gaffney has recently reminded us, the depletion of 'social capital' seems well underway in Ireland also, leading to anxiety being expressed at the weakening sense of 'community' solidarity (whatever level of social aggregation we recognise as a 'community'), and to demands that new forms of social bonding be devised to suit the times and the technology in which and with which we must live as human beings with a sense of dignity and agency.[2]

Again, there are specifically Irish features of this more general predicament of advanced 'western' societies – rural depopulation, with its consequences of social anaemia and institutional decay or shut-down (bank branch, post office, creamery, school, local football team, even regular religious service). Urban sprawl, combining inner-city deprivation and monumental 'officification' with a suburban wilderness of dwellings without adequate communal supports or hospitable sites of socialisation, is the other side of rural depopulation.

If we accept, as I do, that these are real and not phantom issues (for all that they may have elements that have been perennial problems in our modern world since the beginnings of the outset of the great waves of industrialisation, urbanisation, mobility and modernity), then we must begin our consideration of the issues of power, powerlessness, decision-making, and the need to understand and to have some control of our lives, with a brief attempt at historicising our current state or predicament.

There have been significant developments, conceptual and structural, in Ireland since the late 1980s, in the efforts at addressing these issues of powerlessness, empowerment, exclusion and inclusion.[3] The overall global movements that have prompted and, to a degree, shaped these developments in Ireland have complex ideological roots, but we must mention in particular the women's liberation movement (with its fundamental revolutionary agenda of equality – 'bread and roses'); the global ethical agenda that has emerged from a broad critique of the 'economic growth' paradigm of human happiness, in the light of the evidence of vast wealth-creation being accompanied by unprecedented and horrific immiseration (all now immediately and starkly communicable through the global technology of communications); and the debate on 'responsibility' for the environment.

Then there are the specifically Irish circumstances that must be noted. Firstly, we must mention the 'social partnership' model of national development since 1987; a consensus approach in addressing the economic and, by extension, the social crisis of the 1980s (public finances, debts, unemployment levels, etc.). This neo-corporatist model of national planning and development (preceded and informed in the case of each successive 'national agreement' by a NESC report produced by experts and the social partners), represents a significant development in our structures and forms of governance, as well as in our thinking regarding the prerequisites for and the processes of development. In short, representative democratic government has been joined (some might argue eclipsed) by new neo-corporatist structures for national development (economic and, in time, more explicitly social planning, from 1987 to the present time.)

But the concept of social partnership – in all its ramifications – has not been confined to such term-plans at national level. During the past fouteen years there have been other crucial developments in the concept and operation of social partnership at other levels and in different domains of public policy. The concept of partnership (a potentially empowering concept) was extended and refined, and applied in the formulation and implementation of key aspects of social policy. It stimulated the discussion of 'social inclusion' and 'social exclusion': who were entitled, and who *de facto* were to be participants in the social partnership project of State-led development? It raised the question of what structures are best calculated to advance social inclusion. It focused attention on the institutions (the structures and conventions) through which these transactions to arrive at a consensus on 'social partnership' were and are conducted – who devises these institutions and practices, interrogates them, evaluates them, and by what criteria?

It is at this junction, where 'bottom-up' development or sectional interest advocacy and mobilisation has met top-down government or state-sponsored partnerships, that a good deal of change and innovation has taken place. This has not simply happened within the elevated confines of the formal national agreements/partnerships; it has, rather, permeated a wide expanse of the environment in which social policy in particular, and government policy in general, is formulated. Thus, for example, the *consultative* dimension of policy formulation has become much more evident and *formally elaborate* in Ireland during the past decade or so than in earlier decades. Examples might be cited from many different areas, together involving a broad range of forms of public consultation, for example in education, health, the environment, the arts (including broadcasting).

The procedures adopted for this kind of consultation have, as I say, become increasingly visible and formally elaborate – public meetings, forums, submissions to government commissions or enquiries, set-piece pre-budget meetings and discussions (with the media providing extensive, if still selective, coverage). Facilitating some form of consultative or popular involvement (feed-in or feed-back) into the policy domain (formulation, implementation, evaluation) has resulted in other forms of 'consultation' emerging, with a declared intention of meaningful involvement/empowerment of groups, interests or members of the general public in the decision-making process – focus groups, public hearings, consultation with identified interest or user groups, surveys and questionnaires, opinion sampling; monitored pilot projects with subsequent publication and public discussion of the results. The provision of information is an important dimension of this increased 'participatory' culture. At a later stage, policy and advisory committees are seen as having a more participatory edge than mere consultation; and at the end of the day there is, of course, the final arbitration of public opinion through referendum on fundamental constitutional issues (though the experience on the PFP was a revealing moment, in terms of indicating the limits of government enthusiasm for a plebiscitary-style form of public decision-making on selective, politically-sensitive issues; the abortion issue is perhaps the most obvious case of this kind).

The impetus for these developments has come from various sources, but here in Ireland, the National Economic and Social Forum (NESF) has been an important influence, both as exemplar and as sponsor of innovation in devising new forms of 'participatory' democracy in decision-making.

Some of this more 'consultative' disposition in policy-formulation is also evident at local government level, in terms of facilitating public scrutiny of and debate on the county development plans, or specific projects in the development of the physical environment/infrastructure – roads/bypass, waste management plans, etc.

The significance of this new 'consultative' dimension of public policy (the widening arc of consultation, the deepening wedge of involvement) is, of course, open to different (and conflicting) interpretations. On the one hand, it may be taken at face value, as a genuine attempt to ascertain views and facilitate meaningful public access, in structured ways, for groups or individuals, to the formulation and, as appropriate, the implementation and evaluation of public policy. On the other hand, there is a view among sections of the public (one hears it casually or punctuating radio phone-ins and other forms of *vox pop*) that these rituals of consultation are no more than a cynical and manipulative exercise (perhaps with a limited therapeutic value!), a tactic to give the appearance of listening to and heeding the views of the public, while all the time merely managing the effective communication of decisions already taken (by experts, officials, planners, accountants of the State or local government, as a result of private discussions/agreements held with a person or persons unknown, or at least undisclosed to the public). Now, in the current climate, not even the most trusting among us should be surprised or outraged at the evidence of public cynicism on this particular issue. The disclosures at the various tribunals and at the Public Accounts Committee have melted any lingering public innocence as to how decisions were actually made and favours dispensed, in recent times at least, in areas where there seemed to be some procedures for 'open' and transparent public discussion and for due process in the public interest.

I will return briefly to this issue of trust in the value of structures of 'participatory' democracy before concluding this essay. But, for the moment, I wish simply to draw attention to the innovations (in terms of structures and forms) that have been a feature of the past ten or fifteen years. I would also add that the evidence suggests that the discussion of these new developments by leaders of the voluntary and community sector (as evidenced by conferences/seminars, public statements and publications) is increasingly theoretically informed while at the same time being empirically grounded in the realities of the Irish experience 'at local level'.

The more fundamental issue of the framework or paradigm within which the notion of the good life or 'social good' is being thought and talked about has also been addressed in a challenging and radical way by a number of groups and individuals working in the non-State sector in Ireland, in which I would include the universities. These Irish voices challenging the dominant paradigm of quantifiable economic growth being synonymous with or an infallible yardstick of social good, are, of course, part of a wider community throughout the world, questioning the equation of economic growth with development (some on ethical grounds, others on environmental, others still on the grounds of political order and efficiency).

But what is significant, I think, is that this debate has become firmly embedded in the discussion of public policy (in terms of visionary or long-term social values and ideas), and that it is engaging an ever-widening circle of thinkers and 'practitioners' involved in community development, social care and, more directly 'political' activity in the area of active citizenship (lobbying, etc.). I have already mentioned the importance of the NESF in extending the debate on social inclusion and in generating new thinking on new forms of governance based on a sophisticated espousal of the concept of 'active citizenship'. In terms of contributing constructively to this growing debate on sustainable growth and the concept of human progress and social justice, I could (and perhaps should) have mentioned voluntary bodies, such as certain environmental protection groups, elements within the Trade Union movement, groups involved in combating poverty, the Rural Resource Development project itself. And these are only a sample of the current sources for the critique of the 'economic growth as progress' paradigm. (Even the more technical NESC publications have from time to time begun to engage these fundamental issues of 'social good'.[4])

A feature of the developing debate in this area of 'social vision' has been the prominence within it of some radical religious personnel, involved in 'justice' issues inspired by gospel values; of radical social science scholars (in sociology, law, education, psychology and economics), and of a cluster of highly individual and committed philosophers.[5]

It would be remiss, however, not to mention in particular the contribution to the debate on justice, social inclusion, equality and, most fundamentally, the issue of social cohesion, progress and 'the social good', made during the 1990s by CORI. Indeed, among the most challenging propositions of recent years has been that of Seán Healy and Brigid Reynolds in attempting to provide the basis for a new development paradigm – what they call the paradigm of 'right relationships' – that might encompass global ethical and environmental imperatives, and be based upon an active and responsible exercise or discharging of citizenship. It is worth quoting here their four central categories constituting 'right relationships':

- Relationship with self and God *(interior life)*.
- Relationship with people *(social life)*
- Relationship with institutions *(public life)*
- Relationship with the environment *(cosmic life)*

As they conclude, 'We grow as persons through these four sets of relationships. A just society is one that is structured in such a way as to promote these right relationships so that human rights are respected, human dignity is protected, human development is facilitated and the environment is respected and protected.'[6]

Now, Healy are Reynolds are aware, as we must be, of the need to render these ideas intelligible and operable – so that they do not dissolve or float away as interesting if elusive abstract ideas. But I would suggest that there is less danger of this happening in the coming decade than at any time since the foundation of the State. May I briefly indicate my grounds for taking such an optimistic view.

Firstly, there is a much closer relationship between 'practitioners' and theorists (a more responsive and robustly critical link between theory and practice) than heretofore (the general result of greater numbers involved in the debate, more formal education, more direct contact and debate in conferences, seminars, drawing up proposals, 'critiquing' each other's positions, proposals and tactics). There is sufficient 'critical mass', in every sense of the word, to ensure that ideas do not wither into abstraction: a sufficient number of people, with a broad spectrum of special interests, causes and experience, believe that there is too much at stake – regarding the future of their society – not to try to get the terms of the debate (often colloquially spoken of as 'the bigger picture') right for the consideration and evaluation of whatever issues they themselves may be particularly concerned with. (At a local level, we can see this increasingly in the spread of expert knowledge and competences available to, and availed of by, local groups concerned with environmental matters: the discussion of such issues is more 'informed' at every level.)

Secondly, I think we can point to clear evidence that, however slowly or unevenly it may be happening, new ideas on the issues of exclusion and disempowerment, justice and equality are becoming embedded in, indeed are permeating, official pronouncements and, in certain areas, government policy at the level of political power within the representative political institutions (the Oireachtas, local government). Thus, for example, the issue of 'social inclusion' (first raised as far back as the early 1970s – in the context of the poverty debate at the time), is now firmly embedded in the declared objectives (and the dedicated resources) in wide areas of State policy. The National Plan (to 2006) includes firm commitments and dedicated resources to initiatives in social inclusion. Nowadays, no major/sectoral initiative in social policy is likely to be launched without an explicit commitment to social inclusion being included (e.g., in the areas of adult education, or health promotion, etc.).[7]

I make no judgement or comment on the efficacy of any particular set of government initiatives, or on the adequacy of the resources being provided, or indeed on the appropriateness of the categories of intervention given priority. What I am saying is that the concept of social inclusion as a worthy objective of State (social) policy has penetrated the official mind and the political agenda. (The detailed story of how this was done – the stimulus provided by the women's movement, by European precedents and pressures, by bottom-up 'political' action of various groups, by special Commissions, such as the Social Welfare Commission of 1986, and by the NESF itself since

1993 – needs more careful narrating than space permits in this paper.) But no one can seriously pretend that the climate for the discussion of social policy (and the language in which it is discussed) has not changed in important ways during the past ten to fifteen years.

As with 'social inclusion', so also with the larger issue of 'equality' in society, which has benefited enormously from the widespread interrogation of the theoretical literature on equality by those involved in public policy formulation and implementation, at various levels, in Ireland in recent decades. The expansion of the meaning of equality (in terms of its incarnation in policy objectives and instruments), from a general 'liberal' view in the 1960s of 'equality before the law' and, in terms of social rights, 'equality of opportunity', to a much broader definition is reflected in the recent (1996) formulation of the NESF's four elements of 'equality':[8]

1. Equality of formal rights, opportunities and access
2. Equality of participation
3. Equality of outcome or success
4. Equality of condition

This expanded understanding, though it poses many difficult questions, is a good indication of the way in which the dialogue between social theory and social policy has been enriched in Ireland in recent years. This challenging version of 'equality', while it may have been driven initially by gender issues, will undoubtedly inform the discussion and debate on other aspects of structural 'inequality' in the years ahead (e.g., inequality on racial or ethnic grounds in an increasingly ethnically pluralist Ireland, or inequality based upon geographical location, that is, on the structural deficits of location).

Or, again, to take a final example, let us advert to the general debate on active citizenship, and on the efforts being made to develop new forms of governance (new vehicles for the 'empowerment' of people), striking an acceptable balance between representative democracy (with which we are familiar and whose legitimacy, at least – whatever about its effectiveness – is generally accepted) with more participatory models of democratic participation. Within this debate, the importance of the institutional forms being employed in facilitating 'consultation' and 'participation' of citizens in the decision-making process has been closely examined, and the particular challenges posed and constraints imposed by the institutional form of the consultative or declared participatory structures, have been highlighted (e.g., the actual conduct of a public meeting, the structuring of group discussions, the format of an application form, the classification of significant/relevant information – all such conventions have been the subjects of discussion).

As one study concluded in 1991:

> Institutionalized arrangements are reproduced because individuals often cannot even conceive of appropriate alternatives (or because they regard as unrealistic the alternatives they can imagine). Institutions do not just constrain options: they establish the very criteria by which people discover their preferences.[9]

In short, these arrangements shape the way we think and imagine what is 'realistic', if not indeed what is 'possible'.

This kind of awareness is spreading – though I do not for a moment suggest that everybody in the voluntary sector involved in consultative structures is equally street-wise in these matters – and it is a most valuable acquisition for those hoping to engage purposefully with the apparatus of an historically highly centralised and decidedly secretive State (e.g., for the new mood of engagement, see Department of Social Welfare (1997), *Supporting Voluntary Activity: A Green Paper on the Community & Voluntary Sector and its Relationship with the State*).

The examples I have cited, and the general tenor of my remarks on development in critical thinking and in the politicisation of the community and voluntary sector in recent decades, and indeed on the signs of government responsiveness to the emerging agenda of an active civil society articulating its demands over a range of issues (equality, social inclusion, 'participative' democracy and active citizenship) – the account to date, as I say, has generally been optimistic in tone. I should like to temper this optimism a little, before turning in my concluding remarks to the future, and to some issues that I feel may demand attention in the coming decade (the time horizon of this conference). But first, to the glass half-empty!

In terms of decision-making, the power relationships and structures operating between the national and local (or indeed even sub-national) levels remain seriously defective. The notion of 'balanced regional growth' (a declared objective of development policy at European level for more than three decades, and one regularly echoed by Irish governments throughout that period), has not been seriously engaged. Continuous rural depopulation and continuous over-growth of the Dublin region, have produced predictable if contrasting social crises (social anaemia in one case, congestion and logistical bottlenecks, and a significant degree of social alienation and destructive energy, in the other). The reforms in local government have been disappointingly limited to date – with a very limited developmental role being tagged on to the traditional and limited functions of the county councils and corporations.[10] (Modest initiatives in consultative democracy have been attempted in some areas of local government decision-making, though many elected local politicians, and perhaps more crucially, many local officials/administrators are suspicious of voluntary, 'self-appointed interferers' becoming involved, for example, in aspects of the planning process.)

So far as regional, sub-national structures are concerned, the least said the better. Nobody can seriously pretend that the so-called Border, Midlands and Western 'region' is other than a flag of convenience to maximise European funding under a particular set of income indicators. This 'region' is, literally an opportunistic geographical creation, without historical, logistical, physical or associational meaning. The decision-making structures devised for implementing the National Plan also clearly demonstrate the continuing concentration of real decision-making at the centre of the government/administrative apparatus (notwithstanding some discretion in prioritising expenditure under very limited headings being allowed to the 'regional' authorities).[11] The infrastructural developments proposed in the Plan are likely to excite some revealing demonstrations of how remote from the main sites of decision-making many local communities (villages, parishes, even small towns) feel themselves to be: it is only when flashpoints occur – on a highway or a major waste-management proposal – that the real extent of local anxiety, anger and frustration emerges.

The lack of coherence or integration between various other sub-national or regional institutions or agencies of economic and social policy need not be laboured here (the variations in unit or territorial size between health boards and tourism agencies, for example; or between educational structures and economic development agencies such as the IDA, EI or Údarás na Gaeltachta; to say nothing of the strange and still unexplained fate of SFADCO as a regional development agency). Any attempt to seriously plan for achieving balanced regional development (including rural population retention on sound socio-cultural as well as ecologically persuasive grounds) would demand a radical change of attitudes within our political culture – at least insofar as it relates to key aspects of our system of political representation (where the brokerage role of politicians – county councillor to TD to Minister of State to Minister – is an established way of accessing a centralised government decision-making system).

The ameliorative but limited role of programmes such as LEADER, the ubiquitous 'Task Force' for the employment black-spot hit by the sudden or final shut-down of a single supporting industry: these familiar features of response to serious and systemic weaknesses and patterns of decline in many local communities are indicative of what is wrong with our current approach. The complexity of the issues of community development in areas of demographic decline (requiring reversal) and social decay (requiring renewal) will be well-known to those attending this conference. But it is no harm reminding ourselves of one or two aspects of the problem that clearly demonstrate this complexity.

The application of the concept of equality on *geographical* grounds (as distinct from gender or social class or creed or colour) to the area of education, let us say, would have to contend with the fact that, on the basis of comparative participation rates in third-level education on a county by county basis, some western counties would seem (according to the Clancy Reports) to be well-provided for in terms of opportunity. Yet, looked at more closely, it is clear that, for many communities in these same western counties, high participation rates of their young people in third-level education significantly increases the possibility (if it does not virtually guarantee) that these young people will be lost thereafter to their local areas/communities – as the mismatch of local employment opportunities to educational attainment (and corresponding expectations/aspirations) will dictate that the well-qualified young people will, in the main, be unlikely to return to settle among the communities in which they were born and reared.

There is no easy answer to this dilemma. Certainly I am not for a moment suggesting that participation in third-level education is a bad thing or some kind of Trojan horse in terms of rural depopulation. What I am suggesting is that when we talk of integrated development we are embarking on a complex analysis of difficult data and committing ourselves to difficult choices and decisions. But the incoherence of current structures of decision-making at the macro level in State industrial policy, social infrastructure investment, and general service provision, and between the State and the local (or sub-national) level, renders the task of even comprehending the inter-connectedness of different aspects of State intervention and local needs and desires extremely difficult, to say nothing of the difficulties involved in planning and achieving local development through the empowerment of people in a time when global forces are affecting local circumstances intensely, posing formidable challenges to the effectiveness and capacity of the national State itself.

Conclusion

What prospect, then, does the next decade hold out, and what should we strive for? (A word of caution may be advisable at this point: historians are notoriously poor forecasters, not least because the future – even the immediate future – is rarely, in fact is never, a mere extrapolation from key indicators or directions present or instinct in our current situation and circumstances.) Nevertheless, in contemplating what seems like a relatively modest time-horizon – the next ten years – what are the main issues that need to be addressed if the sense of powerlessness with which I began this essay is to be tackled? (Alienation is one version of this powerlessness, resignation or despair another; frustration, anger and passivity are different responses to it.)

I make a vital assumption that, notwithstanding the increasing intensity of global forces (economic integration, global dimensions to communications, 'culture' and the environment) that shape, and will continue to shape our world and our view of the world in the next decade, and notwithstanding significant deepening that may occur in the integrating structures of the EU (with obvious and not so obvious implications for decision-making and empowerment), I take it that the national State will continue to be a key site in determining the configuration of power relationships for the citizens of this State during the coming decade.

On this assumption, I suggest that some convincing criteria of evaluation – some indicators of effectiveness under a number of headings – will have to be developed for the various new modes of consultation and participation in decision-making that have been tried in recent years. This is an essential and urgent task, if these structures (and those who are working them in good faith) are not to be overwhelmed or demoralised by corrosive public cynicism (and, as I have indicated, the revelations at the Tribunals and elsewhere have encouraged people to expect bad faith and deception in these matters: and this feeling will strengthen if there is not an outcome to these enquiries that demonstrably renders those guilty of wrong-doing accountable). How often have we heard people say, after they have given voice to criticism of some decision or official action or inaction – ' Well, I had my say, anyway, for all the good it will do'. This is not to dismiss the psychological importance of 'having your say'; but it is not enough. Of course, human nature being as it is, comments of this kind may be made even of consultative exercises (meetings, questionnaires, etc.) in which there is a firm and good intention all round to take seriously the views expressed by the public. But it is vital that those who are committed to advancing the practice of active citizenship through wider and more meaningful participation in decision-making in the broad domain of public policy should take steps to ensure that the value of such exercises in consultation can be clearly demonstrated and protected.

With representative democracy (the politicians elected to national or local institutions of political power), we have some indicators of how the public 'value' the system: the level of turn-out, the number of candidates, the intensity of the debate, the evidence for the 'virtuous' functioning of the system (its honour, integrity, freedom from corruption, etc.). But, if RTÉ or the Department of Health holds ten public meetings instead of five, to discuss their plans or to canvass the opinions of the public, how, apart from acknowledging the geographic spread of the sample, can we say that the consultation process went well, that it was 'valuable'? Have we criteria that are robust and subtle enough, specific without being reductionist, for assessing the 'value' to the public – at a local and at a national level – of these particular forms of participatory democracy? ('Do these really make a difference to the process of decision-making? 'might be one way of underlining the issue of evaluation). For example, the Department of Health, or so it seems to me, has been especially active in taking part in many of these new forms of 'empowerment' through information flows, public consultation and discussion of key aspects of the health and caring agenda (e.g., women's health issues). And, yet, there are few areas on which public distress and anxiety is more frequently and trenchantly-expressed (in all media) than in respect of waiting lists, closure of wards, curtailment or termination of 'local' services through rationalization or the imperatives of unit costing or on the grounds of economies of scale. What exactly is wrong, then, and is the consultation process simply irrelevant, inadequate, ineffective, badly-focused? Indicators of the effectiveness of these new forms of participatory democracy ('responsible, active citizenship') will have to be found – while accepting that some voluntary 'activists' may at some point decide that they can exercise greater influence by standing for election and accessing the decision-making process directly through the institutions of *representative democracy.*

On the evidence to date, it is questionable if the current repertoire of structures and modalities mainly operating in the area of social policy for the development of a more participatory form of citizenship have yet gained sufficient credibility to dispel the widespread feeling of powerlessness felt by large numbers of people living in communities in deprived urban as well as deprived rural communities in Ireland. Local government reform (even with recent constitutional recognition of its importance and some modest new functions allocated/permitted) has not been sufficient to encourage local public confidence in the ability of their own 'local authorities' to deal effectively with 'local' problems (e.g., Dublin housing and traffic; waste disposal and management in every corner of the State; not surprisingly, there is talk of American-style popularly-elected executive mayors). The current mechanisms for public consultation in the political process do not seem to be convincing the public at large that they really do have a say – a meaningful say – in determining the forces and the choices that shape their lives and the life of their communities.

The declining level of popular participation in the voluntary and community sector is itself a problem. This is not altogether surprising: people have many calls on their time, 'the private' spheres of transaction and gratification have expanded, the public space for socialisation has contracted; increasingly, many activities traditionally the domain of the 'voluntary' sector are nowadays staffed by waged 'professionals'. Where 'professionals' are involved, the concept of service has a particular meaning for members of the general public.

Indeed, the mobilisation of communities for collective political purposes seems to be increasingly reactive in character and purpose: reacting to decisions (or virtual decisions as they are often perceived) already made, by national or local authorities. Frequently, mobilisation takes place in order to resist the imposition of something or other perceived as a threat: a major road, a superdump or an incinerator; a halting site; a hostel or residence for those classified as socially problematic groups (e.g., offenders, asylum seekers or other 'outsiders').

What is missing in many communities is a rooted and coherent sense of collective responsibility and capacity for building their own community, a coherent vision and comfortably shared version of themselves as a community. And it seems to me that it is in this vital area of vision, values and vocabulary (the language of empowerment) that the main challenge of the coming decade may be found, and it is to this issue that I will now address my concluding remarks.

The most challenging project facing community leaders and political leaders alike in the coming decade will be the creation of a new inspiring language and social vision that goes beyond the valorisation of economic growth as an end in itself and as the hegemonic discourse of human endeavour and human achievement. This task is already being undertaken – as I indicated earlier in this paper – by thinkers and 'doers', in the academy and in the field of community action: new paradigms – particularly the paradigm of right relationships, informed by global ethical and environmental obligations – have been proposed. There is a fruitful debate gathering momentum, in a sense 'from the bottom up', mediated by a coalition of activists and intellectuals and witnesses to conscience in a broken world. This demand for a new paradigm, a new social vision, a worthy answer to the question 'what kind of society are we/do we want to be', will, I am confident, gather support and momentum in the coming decade – just as equality and social inclusion and women's rights have done in recent decades. But the response to this challenge must also come from the top: from the top level of political leadership in particular.

It is customary, but in my view a mistake, to dismiss out of hand the willingness or the intellectual capacity of our political leadership to engage serious, complex and long-term issues of social vision and social development, even at the level of the national State/community. I am inclined not to be so dismissive. There is evidence to suggest a willingness on the part of some political leaders to engage complex and long-term issues of social consequence when the pressure to do so becomes sufficiently compelling. However tardily, there is evidence that the environmental protection/waste management/noxious emissions issue is finally arriving at a point in which hard choices – and politically difficult or contentious decisions – will actually be made by politicians, including Irish politicians.

Likewise, the early stages of the political debate sparked by the Tánaiste, Mary Harney's comment in mid-summer 2000 on Ireland's closer affinities with the American than with the European 'cultural route' to progress suggest that serious questions on visions for Irish society in the future may well elicit serious debate among sections of our political leadership in the years ahead. Other straws in the wind might include Minister Síle de Valera's comments on future European integration and the challenge it may pose for the nation-state and cultural diversity therein; the public comment by a former Taoiseach, Dr Garret Fitzgerald, that there is such a thing as excessive economic growth, and comments by distinguished commentators that it may not be prudent for the IDA to continue on its traditional mission of actively seeking inward investment by transnational industrialists. Serious and interesting questions are being asked in many quarters.

I don't underestimate the challenge facing our political leaders in having to create a new language of social vision that is inspiring but grounded in reality and in achievable goals informed by worthy and humane values. For historical reasons, Irish political leaders may be reluctant to embark upon offering an inspiring vision of and for Irish society, rather than sticking to the safe and quantifiable indices of 'economic progress and prosperity' (as measured and classified in growth terms – GDP per capita, unemployment levels, etc.). The sources of this reluctance and inhibition on the part of our political elite to articulate a social vision are complex and fascinating, and I can do no more than hint at one or two key aspects of the explanation in this paper.

The most striking – and frequently quoted – social vision articulated by a political leader in modern Ireland is De Valera's 1943 St Patrick's day speech, ' The Ireland that we dreamed of'[12]. In recent times, whenever this speech is quoted it is almost invariably in order to ridicule or denounce its sentiments, its language and its images of the 'virtuous society', of a people 'living the life that God desires that man should live'. The crisis of the 1950s, with a stagnant economy and massive emigration, buried De Valera's social vision. The gap between the 'cosy' utopian vision of frugality and the grim reality of the 1950s exodus provoked a bitter backlash. An improved economic performance became the priority, with no-nonsense quantifiable performance criteria being demanded as evidence of economic and social progress. The sacral text of Irish ambition, achievement and progress since the late 1950s has been T. K. Whitaker's *Economic Development* (published in 1958)[13].

In reaction to the language of De Valera's social vision, and also to the excessively severe message of mortification incessantly proclaimed by an authoritarian Catholic Church during the decades of its greatest influence on social thought and practice in the new Irish State, the

Irish people from the 1960s avidly adopted the goals of economic progress and development – measured in conventional terms of GDP per capita, employment levels and growth rates – as the true measure of 'the good society'. Some politicians, it is true, sought to encase the drive for material progress in a broader social vision: one may note Declan Costello's *The Just Society* project of the mid-1960s, or, indeed, the enthusiasm for a humane socialism espoused by elements of the Left (including Labour) in Ireland in the late 1960s. But it is probably fair to say that a general preoccupation with the conventional indicators of a growth economy, and the different political parties basing their competing claims on public support on their declared intentions or proven capacity for 'stimulating' or 'managing' economic growth, have been the dominant themes or features of Irish politics in recent decades. It is only in the light of the phenomenal growth of the Irish economy since the early 1990s that the debate seems to be shifting to more complex choices and social visions for a now clearly 'prosperous' Irish society. It is interesting, for example, that the most recent national agreement between the social partners is called the *Programme for Prosperity and Fairness*. The agenda, and the political language, may be changing.

Indeed, there are encouraging signs that the public mood may be receptive to a fundamental shift in the political rhetoric of national achievement and progress. And, by rhetoric, I do not mean the empty sloganising with which a smart spin-doctor might follow a market-led session or think-in: I mean a deeply felt and carefully worked out public rhetoric of virtue, based on an inspiring social vision. The public criticism of 'poverty in the midst of plenty', both within Irish society itself and shockingly at a global level, is increasingly being articulated in ethical terms: by phone-ins to radio programmes, by authority figures in the judiciary, and by large numbers of citizens from all walks of life, as well as by those (such as religious) who might be expected, by reason of their special vocation, to privilege moral or ethical perspectives in their particular social vision. The neglect of the dignity of people with disabilities or special needs; the evidence of the social landscape of boom-time Ireland well-populated by casualties – from the underage ravaged nomads of our city doorways and alleyways, to those in rural isolation living lives of quiet desperation because of inadequate provision of basic services of care: these realities are increasingly being denounced not as a paradoxical side-effect of the unprecedented prosperity of the Celtic Tiger, nor indeed as an anomaly, but *as a scandal*, a scandal in moral and ethical terms to which our response must be more than the immediate reflex of outrage, guilt or shame. The debate – still in its infancy – on refugees, asylum seekers and immigrants, and the challenge that the newcomers pose to our version of tolerance, justice and 'fair play', has the potential to be enormously positive and to do us great good, if we can keep our sights high.

What I have been suggesting in this essay is that in order to undertake a more radical critique of the sources of this 'scandal' in our society, and to seriously challenge the sense of disempowerment that many people clearly feel in the face of the general state of things, we need to go beyond (indeed to actively subvert and replace) the dominant or hegemonic discourse of recent decades (to which, as I have suggested, we in Ireland were historically conditioned to submit rather thoroughly and uncritically), in which economic growth (as the key indicator of progress towards 'the good society') has provided the matrix for our own vision and version of ourselves; a discourse in which, more latterly, under Anglo-American auspices since the 1970s, society is equated with, and reduced to, a marketplace for demands and desires, for services and supplies, for consumer goods trading as social good.

The language that we – all of us – use is a key sensitive site for this movement towards a more dignified, more humane empowerment of people. This will require a major effort to change from the all-pervasive and incarcerating language of liberal capitalism, which has come to dominate so many domains of our ordinary speech (our ways of describing reality) for more than half a century, but which has become especially pronounced in Ireland in recent decades. Thus, for example, we must insist that a good education – or a good university degree for that matter – is not to be spoken of as 'a quality product', any more than beautiful scenery and friendly people should be described as 'quality tourist products'. Those who are ill or who seek care in a hospital are not 'customers' (in the sense that motorists in the forecourt of a service-station are customers for petrol). Indeed, we should be wary of 'social capital' as a description of the matrix of social relationships, institutions and attention that bonds a community; the cost-benefit analysis of returns on the investment of any kind of capital (including social capital) only has meaning, ultimately, in the context of the commodification of all transactions, including human or social relationships. In short, but crucially, we need to watch our language.

The economic or material base of our living is, of course, a critical element of the base of any society. But the political leadership in Ireland in the coming decade will need to find a vision of society that subsumes the economic base, that is humane and socially integrating. Whether it is to be based on a paradigm of right relationships or some variant thereof, it will need to have a strong emancipatory edge, to be liberationist in tone (liberation from fear, from want, from oppression, from discrimination); and its commitment and convictions will need to be carried into practices and structures (inclusive and caring, responsive and responsible, participatory and structurally integrated); policies and structures that seek (however imperfectly, however much requiring constant interrogating, review and renewal) to empower people, living as members of multiple interlocking communities (family, village/neighbourhood, city, county, region, country, global – virtual communities of the internet) – to empower people in these complex and interlocking community relationships so that they may have a meaningful and dignified say, a meaningful sense of human agency, in shaping their own lives and in developing the communities and the environment in which they live.

Political leadership will be vital in meeting this challenge, and, as in any healthy civil society, those who are already converted to this project must play an active part in persuading, convincing, encouraging, evangelising and educating the political leadership for this new and most challenging version of 'social partnership' in the years ahead.

Notes

1. References for this essay have been kept to a minimum, and are intended to indicate interesting further reading as well as sources for direct quotations. Stimulating critiques of liberal capitalism in its latest phase are John Gray, *False Dawn: The Delusions of Global Capitalism* (London, 1998), and Thomas Frank, *One Market Under God* (London, 2000).

2. Maureen Gaffney, 'Invest Now in Social Capital', in the *Irish Times Magazine*, 21 October 2000.

3. Key texts for the study of this debate – texts that significantly influence aspects of the commentary in this essay on 'social inclusion' and 'equality' – are: Suzanne Quin, Patricia Kennedy, Anne O'Donnell and Gabriel Kiely, eds., *Contemporary Irish Social Policy* (Dublin,1999); Gabriel Kiely, Anne O'Donnell, Patricia Kennedy and Suzanne Quin, eds., *Irish Social Policy in Context* (Dublin, 1999); P. Clancy et al, eds., *Irish Society: Sociological Perspectives* (Dublin, 1995); Seán Healy and Brigid Reynolds, eds., *Social Policy in Ireland: Principles, Practice and Problems* (Dublin, 1998, and 1999 reprint.).

4. NESC, *New Approaches to Rural Development* (1994), and NESC, *A Strategy into the 21st Century* (1996).

5. See, for example, Harry Bohan and Gerard Kennedy, eds., *Working Towards Balance* (Dublin, 2000), and Eoin G. Cassidy, ed., *Prosperity With a Purpose: What Purpose?* (Dublin, 2000).

6. Healy and Reynolds, op. cit., p.11.

7. *Ireland: National Development Plan 2000–2006* (Pn.7780. Dublin, 1999).

8. Cited in Healy and Reynolds, op. cit., p.16.

9. Kieran Healy, 'The New Institutionalism and Irish Social Policy', in Healy and Reynolds, op. cit., p. 69. See also Brigid Reynolds and Seán Healy, eds., *New Frontiers for Full Citizenship* (Dublin, 1993)

10. But see *Task Force on Integration of Local Government and Local Development Systems: Report* (Government Publications, Dublin, 1998)

11. *Ireland: National Development Plan 2000–2006,* chapter 10, pp.187-198.

12. Text in Maurice Moynihan, ed., *Speeches and Statements by Eamon De Valera, 1917–1973* (Dublin and New York, 1980), pp. 466-469.
13. In fairness to Dr Whitaker, he himself is in no sense an economic 'reductionist', but a man with a broad humane vision.

REBUILDING SOCIAL CAPITAL:
RESTORING THE ETHIC OF CARE IN IRISH SOCIETY

Dr Maureen Gaffney

Over the past quarter century, Irish society has been transformed, almost beyond recognition. And what is most astonishing – and as yet unexplained – is the almost indecent speed with which this transformation was accomplished. Consider this. A man who was part of the town committee that invited the Christian Brothers to set up in his community lived to see the day when the local Christian Brothers school closed for good because of lack of vocations. The era of Irish education as synonymous with, indeed virtually inconceivable without, the involvement of the religious orders was over.

That astonishing turnaround was replicated in virtually every area of Irish life – fertility patterns, religious observance, unemployment, emigration, economic progress. From a barely standing start in the mid-1980s, with the public finances in crisis and mass unemployment and emigration, we have become competitive in a global market. We have become a self-confident voice in the world. I salute that progress.

In the human life cycle, there is always a 'golden moment' when an individual reaches the end of a period of striving. A personal agenda has been successfully completed. Then, there is often a feeling of restlessness, even vague discontent: 'Is this it? Now that I have it, is it what I thought it would be? Is this what I really want to do with my life?' If they are wise, individuals will attend to those feelings and engage in a period of stocktaking, working their way back to the fundamental question: 'Just what was the dream or vision I had for my life and what do I want from it now?' If they don't do that, two things can happen. They can keep striving, but now in a less personally committed and satisfying way and burn themselves out. Or they can give up and enter a period of personal stagnation.

I believe that Irish society has now reached that 'golden moment'. It is now time for a reappraisal. At a time of unprecedented boom, many people feel an unexpected unease, which surfaces more and more in conversations about 'quality of life'. Behind the urgent concerns about health, house prices, childcare, political corruption, I believe there is a more indefinable new worry – that the old ways of belonging that characterised Irish society are slipping away and being replaced by an edgy, stressed-out individualism – especially among the young. We have become uneasy about the quality of our connection with each other.

I will try to sketch out the high-pressure, high-change global context within which Irish society is now operating. Second, I will look at the challenges we now face. Third, I will ask what kind of vision can energise our rebuilding of social capital.

Setting the Context: Globalisation and the Information Society

These two terms now trip easily off our tongues. They are, of course, related. Yet, it is only now that we are beginning to fully grasp the sheer scale of the revolution that engulfs us all that is embedded in those terms. Futurist Alvin Toffler has labelled our current transition to the information age as the 'Third Wave', suggesting that it may ultimately be as significant as the last two waves in human history – the first in prehistoric times, when we made the move from hunter-gatherer to agricultural societies, the second during the industrial revolution, when we moved from agricultural to industrial societies.

What are the Characteristics of this Third Revolution?

Speed. As writer Thomas Friedman so vividly puts it: The world, as we now know it, is just ten years old. Most people had never heard of the internet in 1990, very few used email or had mobile phones. In the era of globalisation, the defining criterion is speed – speed of commerce, speed of travel, speed of communication and speed of innovation. The pace and reach of electronic and technological revolution in the past decade is simply astonishing. For example, from the time of its invention in 1890, it took the telephone 67 years to reach 75% of American households. The car was invented in 1908 and took 52 years to reach 75% of households. It took the radio just 14 years to reach that and the television a mere 7. We have not yet experienced the full extent of the scale, pace and reach of the internet. Advances in microchip technology have resulted in the doubling of computing power every eighteen months – the so-called 'Moore's Law' – and this is set to continue and accelerate over the next thirty years. According to Bill Gates, the only thing they know for sure at Microsoft is that every one of their products will be obsolete in four years. As Klaus Schwab of the Davos World Economic Forum once observed: 'The world used to be a place where the big ate the small. Now the fast eat the slow.'

Relentless competitiveness. Joseph Schumpeter, the guru of globalisation, coined the term 'creative destruction' to describe the need in a modern economy for the perpetual replacement of products and services with more efficient ones. Only those who stay one step ahead of the competition will survive. Or as Andy Grove, the former Intel CEO, puts it, 'only the paranoid will survive'. Gary Hamel, formerly of the Harvard Business School, refers to the vulnerabilities of what he calls (in the business context) 'the complacent incumbents' – those organisations who believe that their place in the world is assured. These are the organisations who make some changes under duress, and then think 'Well, that's OK now, we can go back to normal'. But in the global era, there is no going back to normal.

The breakdown of barriers. The life blood of the information society is the free flow of information. Thus, anything that gets in the way of that free flow of information has to go. That is why hierarchies of all kinds – corporate, religious – are crumbling. That is why the media are now so powerful.

Empowerment of the individual. That free-flow of information has empowered individuals. Freedom of choice has exploded, intensifying the already historical shift towards individualism. Individualism carries with it a strong emphasis on rights, autonomy, freedom. Personal and social oppression are the enemies of individual freedom and so it is not accidental that the so-called liberal agenda has such powerful cultural legitimacy behind it.

A focus on services. In business, services have replaced manufacturing as a source of wealth creation. Similarly, in the case of politics and voluntary organisations, a focus on providing innovative and appropriate 'services' has replaced the old-style business – representing people or 'charity'. Service is increasingly defined as 'a solution to a problem' or 'something that works'. Increasingly, we apply the same criterion to our personal lives.

If these are the characteristics of the third revolution, the criteria of success in this new world, then Irish society has been exquisitely in tune with this modern zeitgeist.

The Challenges Ahead

Like all revolutions, there is a downside to this one. In my view, the greatest challenges facing Irish society are as follows:

- the growing inequality
- the relentless pushing to the margins of people who don't fit into the competitive straitjacket of the new thrusting, competitive Ireland
- the rise of a kind of unthinking materialism
- the unprecedented level of distrust and cynicism about authority of all kinds
- the new centrality of work in people's lives that is pushing the work of caring to the margins

These are, if you like, the unintended consequences of our success. They are not the *inevitable* consequences of that success. But, if left untended, they will not automatically correct themselves and will corrode civic society.

The concept of social capital may be a useful point of departure around which to organise our thinking about some of the 'problems of success' Irish society now faces, providing an intellectual umbrella under which a wide range of roles and relationships can be examined – from the larger-scale public role of individual and corporate citizen to the small-scale intimate relationships in families.

Social Capital

Social capital is a term that was recently revived by sociologists and political scientists to mean a society's stock of shared values – such as trust, honesty, reciprocity, empathy, the keeping of commitments. These values enable people to communicate with each other and to enter into any kind of sustainable partnerships or contractual arrangements. We are more familiar with terms like physical capital (land, natural resources) or human capital (education, skill). But social capital is also an essential building block of a society. Social capital is what creates a society as opposed to an economy.

Social capital also refers to those dense networks of connections and mutual obligation between individuals that have always existed in society – informal socialising with family and friends, membership of clubs and voluntary organisations, and helping others.

Social capital finds many expressions.

- active *political engagements* – voting, interest in current affairs, reading newspapers, watching the news/news programmes on TV
- *civic participation* – being a member of a club or association; religious engagement – attending services regularly, involvement in church-based voluntary activity
- *informal social connections* – socialising with friends and neighbours, entertaining friends at home
- *voluntary and community activity*
- high levels of *trust and reciprocity*
- *work-based networks* and friendships

The Decline in Social Capital

In the US and other advanced market economies, there is growing concern about the depletion of social capital. Now that Ireland has joined this élite club and consciously models itself on the US, it may be instructive to look at what has happened to American society over the past half century. Drawing on the huge empirical data banks assembled by American social scientists, Robert Putnam, Professor of Public Policy at Harvard, starkly documents the decline of community in the US.

He outlines how, during the first two-thirds of the twentieth century, Americans took an active role in the political and social life of their communities. They joined clubs, sat on committees, entertained each other in their homes, took an active interest in politics and went out to vote in large numbers. Year by year, they gave increasing amounts of time and money to a wide variety of charitable and community projects. Over three-quarters of them expressed confidence in their neighbours and believed that most people could be trusted. By 1965, America seemed to be entering a golden era of community and civic involvement. But, mysteriously and more or less simultaneously, they began to do all of these things less often.

By the century's end, all had changed. Americans have become increasingly disconnected from family, friends and neighbours. They eat alone more often. They watch of lot of TV. They interact with a much smaller network of people who are increasingly like themselves. They distrust each other more than they used to. Eighty per cent say their fellow citizens have become less civil. Although satisfied with their economic prospects, they worry that their society is not on the right track morally or culturally. And they know the reason: 77 per cent believe that the nation is worse off because of the decline in community.

Ominously, the steepest decline in all kinds of active participation is among young people. What this means, Putman argues, is that the true extent of the decline in involvement will only become apparent as the young generation gradually replaces the older, more civic generations, and becomes more numerous in the population. Compared to their parent's and grandparent's generations (when they were the same age), American adolescents now are less trusting, less inclined to participate, more cynical about authority, more self-centred and more materialistic – emphasising the personal and private over the public and collective. It is as if, Putnam muses, this generation was exposed to some anti-civic X-ray that permanently and increasingly made them less likely to connect with each other.

But does the decline of social capital matter? Yes, the evidence says, not just for the society at large, but for families and individuals.

A trusting society. High social capital creates a more trusting society because being part of a dense network of connection produces a belief that people in general can be trusted to behave in a decent and caring way. In turn, that generalised trust creates a sense of shared identity, a feeling of belonging to a real community. It is this trust that enables individuals and groups to move beyond narrow self interest. In the absence of such trust, companies and society generally will increasingly have to rely on 'preventive law' – surveillance, policing – costly and negative ways of protecting self-interest. The commentator Francis Fukuyama argues that only those societies with a high degree of social trust will be able to create the flexible, large-scale business organisations that are needed to compete effectively in the new global economy and that social capital may become as important as physical or intellectual capital in the rapidly changing economies in the twenty-first century.

Economic prosperity. A growing body of research shows that where trust and social networks flourish, individuals, companies, neighbourhoods and whole societies prosper.

Safe neighbourhoods. Neighbourhoods with strong social and civic participation have less crime.

Physical and psychological health. Study after study shows that social connectedness, having links with friends and with the larger community, is one the most powerful determinants of individual health and well-being for all socio-economic groups. And lack of social connection has a negative influence that rivals that of the old faithfuls – smoking, obesity, high blood pressure and lack of exercise. Social connectedness also affects our psychological well-being. We all know that doubling your income or being married increases happiness generally. But a more unexpected finding is that regular club attendance, doing voluntary work, entertaining your friends at home even once a month, or attending a religious service twice a month – all these rival marriage and affluence as predictors of happiness. For example, suppose you are not a member of any organisation or group and then you decide to join one. According to Putnam, joining up should, on average, cut in half your risk of dying over the next year. Similarly, if you are a smoker and belong to no group, joining a group may be as good for your health as giving up smoking. The relationship between social connectedness and psychological health is even more dramatically illustrated in the case of depression and suicide. Severe depression is now ten times more prevalent in the US than it was fifty years ago, and strikes a full decade earlier in life on average than it did a generation ago. This rising tide of depression and suicide – described by psychologist Martin Seligman as an epidemic – is not just the response to a more stressful modernity. Its explosive growth is mainly among the young. Adolescent suicide increased by 40 per cent in the US from 1970–1990 and by similar amounts in other economically advanced economies. What is most remarkable, as Putnam shows, is that the spread of depression and suicide exactly coincided with the decline in all forms of social and civic engagement, especially among the young, over the last thirty years.

Child and adolescent welfare. In communities where people trust each other, join organisations, volunteer, vote and socialise with friends and neighbours, in comparison to communities that do less of all of those things but are otherwise similar (e.g., income and educational levels, etc.), children and adolescents fare better. Whether it is measured in terms of children's physical and psychological health; their educational attainment; rate of adolescent drop-out from school; adolescent pregnancies; adolescent crimes, Putnam shows that the link with social capital indicators is as close to perfect as you find in the social sciences. In fact, a lack of social capital is second only to poverty in its devastating effects on children and adolescent welfare.

What Accounts for the Decline in Social Capital?

In a careful trawl through the substantial social science research on American lifestyle and attitudes, Putnam identifies the possible causes: increasing time and work pressures, particularly on dual career families; living in sprawling suburbs; and, most significantly, the exponential increase in TV viewing. TV viewing in the US is now more than 50 per cent higher than it was in the 1950s. The average American now watches roughly four hours of television every day. More significantly, the way they watch television has changed. As the number of television sets increases in each household, more and more television viewing is done alone. For children aged 8–18, more than a third is done alone. The proportion of people who now say that they will watch 'whatever's on' has also risen dramatically. Twenty years ago, the number of selective viewers outnumbered the habitual viewers by more than three to two. Now the proportions are reversed.

Moreover, if you divide those who are heavy TV watchers (half of all Americans) and compare them to the light watchers, there are remarkable differences. Heavy watchers spend less time with friends, are less interested in politics, give blood less, express more road rage, and are more socially isolated. And these differences hold across different socio-economic groups. What you watch on television is also significant. More time spent watching news programmes is associated with active social and community engagement. In contrast, more time spent watching soap operas, game shows, and daytime talk shows – which constitute a massive and growing share of television watching – is associated with disengagement.

And when they are not working or watching TV, Americans are driving, mainly alone. The average American suburb dweller now spends more time driving to work and to out-of-town shopping malls than they do on cooking or eating, and more than twice as much as they spend with their children. After all this striving, it is hardly surprising that such couples report that they spend more time on personal relaxation, mainly watching TV, videos or shopping – what Putnam calls 'zoning out' – than on active social and community engagement.

Combined, these factors have contributed to the relentless privatisation of lifestyle – the retreat into so-called 'life-style enclaves' – ever smaller and more homogeneous social worlds – at the expense of participation in the larger public community. American society has also become increasingly materialistic. In 1975, when asked to identify the elements of the 'good life', 38% of American adults chose 'a lot of money' and the same proportion said 'a job that contributes to the welfare of society'. In 1996, the proportions were 63% and 32% respectively. As in all social science research, it is difficult to work out exactly what is cause and what is consequence in any major social change. But the data is strong enough to conclude that those factors identified by Putnam, in combination and feeding off each other, constitute the 'anti-civic' X-ray that permanently eroded the sense of belonging in US society, and have had their most concentrated effect on the young.

Social Capital in Irish Society

Irish society is generally regarded as rich in social capital. Traditionally, religion and politics were the main sources of social capital and we in Ireland were fortunate to have an abundance of both, generally of a very high quality. The convulsions of the last decade should not be allowed to obscure that. But even the most optimistic of observers would be hard put to argue that Irish society is not being buffeted by the same forces identified by Putnam in American society.

In many ways, Putnam's portrait of American society back in 1965, rich in social capital, resembles Irish society now. Or maybe Irish society two years ago. I think at least some of the symptoms of depleted social capital are evident, raising the troubling possibility that as a society (like most advanced western societies) we are spending our social capital without building it up again; raising the troubling question of whether the very runaway success of the Celtic Tiger is undermining our social connectedness, squandering our social capital?

In the absence of sound data, it is, of course, difficult to get a clear picture. In addition, as we see from the US experience, such depletion in social capital is often masked because it is so concentrated among the young and will not be evident until the generation formed in a different Ireland are gradually replaced by the Celtic Tiger generation.

Broadly, there are two kinds of responses to the challenges ahead. The pessimists believe that the loss of belief in all kinds of authority, particularly in politics and religion, the traditional sources of social capital, will inevitably lead to more social isolation and disconnectedness, which will ultimately destroy social solidarity. The problem with this view is that it often ends up as blinkered nostalgia for a golden age that existed only in some people's imaginations. The forces that created our social capital had a dark underbelly. There is no going back.

The optimists, on the other hand, argue that social capital is simply being built in a new way: by new civic institutions based on choice rather than obligation, sustained by a kind of enlightened self-interest rather than by religion or old-style patriotism. People nowadays, they point out, form networks of friends and allies based on choice rather than family or neighbourhood connections. They point to the strength of the voluntary and community sector. And there is truth in this position.

But it is a complex picture. For example, data from the Volunteer Resource Centre is reassuring. They find strong support for voluntary activity among Irish people – 94% believing that voluntary work encourages people to become more actively involved in society. Approximately 33% of the adult population still volunteers, 60% of Irish young people say they are prepared to volunteer for third-world organisations. Yet, voluntary organisations and political parties say they are experiencing increasing difficult in securing committed volunteers. Could it be the case, as in the US, that volunteering is largely concentrated among the older generation and that as they become too old to be active in the community, they are not being replaced by a younger cohort of volunteers?

More fundamentally, it may not be possible for networks based on choice to substitute for sustainable communities. Precisely because they are based on self-interest, people can slide in and out of such elective networks as their self-interests change, so these groupings are necessarily more transient, more utilitarian, and may not have sufficient commitment to keep them going when times get rough.

Such networks are selective. Thus, people in such networks get together with those who are similar to themselves – a common professional or sporting interest – and necessarily exclude those who are very different. This in itself is a form of social capital – so-called bonding capital. But to build a community, you also need to reach across boundaries such as age, class, income – so-called bridging social capital. Relying only on elective networks can result in a kind of moral miniaturisation (i.e., 'this is what works for me') and a loss of the connection to the bigger picture. Finally, connection based on choice and enlightened self-interest necessarily works better when you are young, healthy and relatively powerful than when you are marginalised by poverty, age or disability.

Even when groupings based on self-interest do good work, I believe there are subtle but significant differences between doing good because it is in your self interest to do so (e.g., starting a sporting or self-help group) and doing good based on commitment to a deeper value – what in old-fashioned terms might be described as practising virtue for its own sake. I believe that actions that are motivated by a deep purpose or basic value (for example, commitment to social justice) are imbued with a different kind of energy – more passionate, more altruistic, more capable of transcending the inevitable frustrations, more likely to end in coherent action. And there is sound psychological evidence to back that up. Individuals and organisations (including business organisations) that can tap into deeper values that transcend their immediate self-interest are more resilient and happier than those that don't.

I believe that we in this society can take a cautiously optimistic view of the future. Because of our size, and the strong tradition of social solidarity, Irish society is still very intimate and connected. But the challenges I outlined earlier have to be faced. In our rush to embrace change, old ways of connecting have been weakened. Reliable new ways have yet to be forged.

But the process of regenerating social capital is complex and difficult. It is rather like trying to rebuild a damaged ecology; all the interdependence between flora and fauna that was once natural, effortless, unconscious, now has to be painstakingly reconstructed, often with only partial knowledge of the micro-processes required.

When one set of norms for generating social capital (traditional values) is in decline or destroyed, another set will not automatically take its place. For that to happen, a society, or at least some influential and vocal members of society, have to realise that the old order is indeed gone and that what is required is a project for value regeneration that will replenish the social capital. But that regeneration must be in tune with the modern zeitgeist, in tune with their dreams. Above all, it needs to be underpinned by a vision that unites the players and a clear and coherent set of practical actions that will deliver that vision. There are interesting examples of how this happened at other historical periods.

At the time of the last great revolution, the industrial revolution, society moved from an agricultural to an industrial base, creating a major disruption in values and norms, evident in rising social disorder and moral confusion. Francis Fukuyama describes how the Victorians responded to the depletion of social capital that they saw happening around them and set about forming a radical movement to deliberately create new social capital – in the form of new social rules and values. It was an extraordinarily successful movement, transforming the great mass of illiterate agricultural peasants and urban poor into a stable working class with a sense of themselves, a set of coherent values and rules to live by. At the core of this movement was the inculcation of what we now call Victorian values – control of impulses and respectability – values that then had a crucial role to play in the creating of a civil society. Today, the movement to create and rebuild social capital will of necessity require a different vision, a different set of values. What might those be? I suggest that the ethic of care might be one.

A Vision for the Future: Revaluing the Ethic of Care

I borrow the concept of the ethic of care from the Harvard psychologist Carol Gilligan. She used the terms 'ethic of justice' and 'ethic of care' to describe the typically different ways that men and women understood and structured the relationship between self and others. I think the same concepts can be applied to how societies structure the relationship between the individual and the larger community.

Gilligan (and other researchers) have found that men, for psychological and perhaps biological reasons, place more emphasis on being separate, different and independent of others, while women place more emphasis on being the same as, connected to and close to others. Moreover, Gilligan also found gender differences in two other basic dimensions of relationships – power and care.

Men tend to be more preoccupied by the element of power in relationships than women are. Thus, compared to women, their imagination tends to be more rivetted by the idea of competing rights, the danger of oppression, the importance of fairness and fair rules and procedures. This orientation gives rise to what Gilligan terms the ethic of justice. Women, on the other hand, tend to be more preoccupied by the element of care in relationships – being responsive to individual need, attending to the context of other's dilemmas, sensitive to the danger of abandonment and isolation and to the importance of finding inclusive solutions for all the players in a relationship – what Gilligan calls the ethic of care. Gilligan's research also suggests that moral maturity involves the capability to use both the justice and the care perspective.

Yet, because men have for so long shaped the world, their values and their orientation to the justice perspective have prevailed in almost every sphere. Societies, not by conspiracy, but simply by default, have adopted male psychology as the norm for regulating societies and for standards of success and maturity. Thus, competing rights, autonomy, and control are considered the key concepts, rather than responsiveness to need and inclusion. Thus, the quintessential moral dilemma at a personal or societal level is typically defined as competing rights that require formal and abstract principles for their resolution, involving the most prestigious institutions in society: government, the law, the Churches. Moral problems arising from conflicting responsibilities, and requiring contextual understanding, tend to be seen as of a lesser and messier quality, belonging to the private realm, to be resolved by social workers and the voluntary and community sector.

So preoccupied have we become by the rights perspective that we are in danger of excluding the notion of human dependency from the equation altogether. But dependency is part of the human condition. And those who are dependent need care. And care needs intimacy and contact, so that we are alert to the cues that the dependent person is giving us, so that we can respond to their needs.

How might it be different? We place such value on autonomy, rights, rules and procedures that status in our society is largely coming to be measured by the degree of autonomy an individual can achieve from obligations and intrusions. If we were more focused on the ethic of care, on the other hand, we would place more societal value on the forming and maintenance of close intimate relationships with others, on connection for its own sake. From this perspective, success and status would also be measured by the degree of closeness achieved, by the fulfilling of responsibilities to others.

Because we so value the ethic of power, we place concomitant value on taking the role of the 'generalised other' as a way of solving moral dilemmas. That is, standing back and invoking general principles abstracted from human relationships. Informed by an ethic of care, we would focus more on taking the role of the 'particular other', on 'knowing' the other in a more feeling way, by being able to see the world from his/her perspective. That kind of knowing lends itself to devising more sensitive responses, more attuned to the particular circumstance of the situation.

Focused on the ethic of power, we tend to prioritise social problems that primarily arise from conflicting rights and to judge 'good' solutions as those based on rights and rules. Using an ethic of care, we are more likely to prioritise social problems that arise from conflicting responsibilities and to judge as good those solutions that rely on developing an understanding of personal responsibility to self and others.

Focused on the ethic of power, we define the ever-present danger as the possibility of interference with or from others. Focused on the ethic of care, we are more likely to define danger as the possibility of exclusion or omission, of not responding to others in their personal hour of need.

Gilligan found that the most morally mature people used both the ethic of power and the ethic of care to resolve their dilemmas and were able to move fluidly between the two. So too with society. The nature and complexity of the moral dilemmas facing modern societies are such that they cannot be effectively dealt with using only a justice perspective. If we want to sustain a real community, we have to engage with the complexity of real people and real situations. That will require an ethic of care as well. Relying only on the ethic of justice with its focus on rights and rules may become a justification of indifference and lack of concern.

Gilligan, in her research on individual moral dilemmas, traced the consequences of using only one moral perspective. Her observations could equally apply to how societal problems are dealt with. An ethic of justice sensitises us to the fact that inequality inevitably adversely affects *all* parties in a relationship – and that includes citizens in an unequal society no less than partners in an intimate relationship. But this realisation can be merely formal and intellectual, and those informed exclusively by an ethic of justice are in danger of ending up at a psychological distance from others. Thus, *intimacy* with the reality and context of others' lives becomes the critical experience, making it possible to see both sides of a relationship, to see that others' experiences of situations are truly different from their own; to discover the effects of our actions on others, as well as the cost to ourselves. The challenge is to turn attention from the logic of formal rules to the *consequences* of choice.

An ethic of care sensitises us to the fact that exclusion is destructive for all parties in a relationship. Being responsive to others' needs in a caring way is an intimate act. But the danger here is that the self gets lost and desire and choice, the well-springs of effective action, get masked. Endlessly responding can result in avoidance of necessary conflict and therefore in confusion about where responsibility lies. Thus, the critical balancing experience is not intimacy but *choice*, which provides the opportunity to delineate the balance of responsibilities in relationships.

Being predominantly influenced by an ethic of care does not mean we are constantly consciously choosing to act in a particular way. It simply means that we approach our choices with a set of expectations (that are often out of conscious awareness) about what cues to attend to, with a set menu of acceptable actions to take.

The task now is to develop a critical awareness of the pressures driving us towards autonomy rather than attachment; towards choice rather than commitment; towards fair exchange rather than trust; towards control rather than understanding; towards rights rather than responsibilities. Autonomy, choice, fair exchange, control and rights are the vocabulary of individualism, or the ethos of justice. Attachment, commitment, trust, understanding and responsibility are the vocabulary of a more connected way of being in the world.

CONCLUSION

In this first year of the new millennium, at a time of unprecedented wealth, we may 'choose' not to care. We may invest more and more of our lives in material achievement and autonomy rather than relationships. We may choose to live in 'lifestyle enclaves', segregated by income and education from those who are not like us. We may choose to 'zone out' in front of the TV or drive alone, and not to care about the larger society. But we should be aware that our cumulative choices may be silently and invisibly eroding the quality of Irish life. If we fail to care, history, and our children, will judge us harshly.

Or we can choose to create a more morally mature and caring society. When the Victorians had identified what values needed to be restored to private and civic life, they found a way of promoting a coherent picture of what was desired at every level. The result was that nobody was in any doubt about what it meant to be a decent, law-abiding, non-self-indulgent person in every arena of their lives. We too must find a way to articulate the ethic of care in a way that touches peoples' lives in a real way. So that people can imagine and experience what acting in a caring way means. If we are successful, the concept of caring will stop being empty rhetoric, a flabby aspiration. Instead, it will tap into and develop the cardinal civic virtues that are essential for the common good – the generous impulse, the readiness to be compassionate, the readiness to modulate self-interest, the sense of fair play, the sense of duty. What is needed is an organisational mechanism, a connective tissue that will unite these civic virtues into an effective, coherent force for the pursuit of justice and social solidarity.

Rise of Science, Rise of Atheism: Challenge to Christianity

Bill Collins

Religion is important for most and at the same time it is irrelevant. We live in an age, especially in the United States, when religion and religious practice is a strong, persistent and ongoing concern. Religious language is pervasive in our political discourse. A day does not go by when at some moment, somewhere, through some medium, some kind of religious message is being transmitted with a frequency and intensity that sometimes is simply overwhelming. Starting from the Catholic side, there is of course Mother Angelica, and moving from there almost every denomination appears to be represented. Just by turning on the TV on any given Sunday it seems very obvious that religious messages are getting out to the people and the word is being made known to as many people as want to hear in whatever guise it may appear. To say the very least, there are few among us who have not heard about religion and the truths it is supposed to bring. In my own area of the world one very big denomination had even taken a kind of county by county census of the state in which they had determined, in a manner I have yet to understand, how many people had been saved, in order to target the appropriate areas for evangelical work. Interestingly, it seemed that on a per capita basis, those counties with universities and large urban populations appeared to be in need of the most work. Polls however do report widespread support for religious belief, in both the sense of assent to what are taken to be the important truths of religion, as well as extensive and high levels of financial support for religious institutions. In the day-to-day marketing sense, there is a healthy religious diversity in the United States. Most people, most of the time, express the right attitudes towards religion and religious practice, and it would appear that God is alive and well, serving as a focal point for most people's values and behaviour. Yet, I shall argue that actually nothing could be further from the truth of the matter, that in the United States (and I would suspect, making the necessary allowances for history – a big enough jump – the same is true of the European community), churches and religious practice are accepted as important parts of community life but, if the truth were to be told, they have no bite, no real impact in the sense of presenting insight into the character of the world and thereby being able to offer some sense of how things really are and thus providing guidelines for action, both individual and social, that are grounded in what is real as opposed to how we might feel about them.

Let me give an example. On a given Sunday in any small Southern town of say less than thirty thousand, there are at least five or six different churchs, all of which are typically filled up. One would clearly have to say, on going through such a town, that religion is a going concern, and truly it is. But a closer examination on any given Sunday of this religious fervour reveals an interesting pattern, one that has clearly been the case in European history from the time of the Treaty of Westphalia, but whose effects have been rather different in the United States. This is the fact that each church draws a particular social type. Look at the cars, look at how the people leaving the church are dressed, but most importantly listen to the different messages that are being presented (you can do this by switching from one religious broadcast to another). An obvious difference would be between High Church Anglican and Baptist evangelicals, though to a practised ear, to someone who had lived in the community, there is as much difference between a Presbyterian and Methodist sermon as there would be between an Anglican and Baptist one.

You might want to stop me here and make the point that this is obvious, because people are different and the message must be presented in a manner that would bring the truth of it to where a given congregation might be. But this argument overlooks the central reality: the flow goes the other way; the message is shaped by the congregation and not the other way round. The different religious perspectives on the death penalty, abortion, justice toward the poor, all of which, it would seem, to have a reasonably common Christian response, are in fact sources of intense disagreement at the level of religious language. And here you will almost inevitably say to yourself (to do so publicly might subject you to social disapproval very like those who, unlike the little boy, saw the naked emperor but discreetly said nothing), well, what can you really expect? Isn't all of this at the bottom no more than, can in fact be no more than, a mere matter of opinion? This of course is precisely the point. Institutional religion, religion in general, religous practice and religous talk are in our time, apparently, no more than matters of opinion reflecting the diversity of our societies, and sometimes, for better or worse, acting to reinforce that diversity with all the consequences that that might entail. The truth of things in general is clearly not to be found here amongst the clamour of 'you must do this, or be like this or behave like this if you wish to be this or that'. In fact, in the United States, religious problems of this sort, that is, those associated with various and sundry imperatives, are resolved simply enough by moving to a more congenial group or staying home and watching television. My point boils down to this: practical atheism is simply the notion that religion is subordinate to society, and whatever reality it might convey is typically to be cast in the language of group identification and group solidarity, that is, in the language of feeling. Religious institutions and religious practice more often than not have to do with group membership and, in particular, what is taking place both within the group and to it, than it does with presenting the actual character of the world. Knowledge, from the religious perspective, is really no more than a matter of opinion. I have mine, you have yours. I know mine to be true and will tolerate yours if the conditions are reasonable for doing so.

The truth of the world, its actual character and what I have to do in it, is the province of another, much more compelling institution, one that we ignore at our peril, and one that, if I attend to it carefully, might make it possible for me to acquire those things that by all accounts bring satisfaction and happiness. If you would allow me to stretch the point a bit, if one attends closely enough, one might hear the old religious promises of happiness being offered and, in many cases, actually delivered.

That institution is, of course, the State. Its impact, what it does and to whom, is real and in no way can it be said that its effects and promises are a mere matter of opinion. These actions represent reality, what actually happens for better or worse to all of us. This is because the State possesses physical power. In fact, it is the purpose of the State to organise and deploy, through a variety of means, the enormous power that always comes about when people learn to work together effectively and well. In the West, the increasing capacity of the State, in tandem with scientific advance (each has in fact promoted the other to their mutual benefit), has created an all but awe-inspiring spectacle of power, affluence and prosperity that is unprecendented in the history of the human race. The State, despite the admonitions and reflections of our politicial philosophers, has enormous autonomy. Using a variety of administrative techniques, and operating under a range of different schemes of justification, the State possesses the power to decide who lives and dies, who will prosper and who will not, who will be free and who will be constrained, who belongs to the group and who will be cast out. It decides what we shall know and what we shall remain ignorant about. The State, in short, whether it be limited or total in its scope, has within it, as the overseer of the community's power, the capacity to set boundaries of our lives that are very real, concrete and specific. Its actions are real. Everything else is pale in comparison. At the risk of perhaps overstating the case, one might say that as one moves further from the reality of State action, from the deployment of community power, the less real one becomes in the sense that what one knows and believes has less and less capacity to represent public knowledge.

Clearly, there are three degrees. The State does not now nor has it in the past been the absolute arbiter of what is real, but my point is that this is the potency, the latency, that lies at the foundation of the State's power. The capacity to act as arbiter of the real, however, accounts for the phenomenon of practical atheism. It has been a major goal of the State to reconcile social conflicts within its borders, and if it is true that religion is primarily a matter of social identification, then any presumably objective religious knowledge must be reduced as much as possible to opinion, as an important means of solving the social conflict problem. The modern State has thus alway had an interest in reducing religious knowledge to opinion. In the United States, this takes the form of promoting diversity, i.e., every one is entitled . . . , etc., and stipulating, sometimes to a ludicrous degree, that there will be no established or dominant religious point of view at any time or in any place. This has the happy effect of giving everyone their own view but diminishing any sense that it is anything more than that – your specific point of view (very clever).

We have reached a point where a summary is in order. The nature of practical atheism is that religion is only superficially about God, the character of the world and how we should be living in it. In reality, religious knowledge has been transformed for the most part into social knowledge, opinion. This phenomenon, practical atheism, parallels the rise of the State. In tandem with the advances of science, the State has become the point of origin for defining the reality of the world and what we should do with respect to it. As the State has increased in power, its influence has extended to the very way in which we have come to understand our world and our place in it. Religion is therefore to be viewed as clearly important to many, but at the same time, irrelevant. On this reading of the meaning of practical atheism, religion should have little, if any, bearing on the the reality of any community-wide problem, and any realistic resolution of such problems must eventually come to terms with practical realities of day-to-day life, which are for the most part ultimately referable, depending upon the character and scope of the problem, to the collective resources of the community, that is, to the State.

The question now before us is, first, how did this issue of practical atheism happen and what, if anything, can be said in reply? My purpose here is not so much to descry the power of the State, nor to wish it away. It is, after all, in my opinion, ubiquitous. The State is the dominant social form, and its voice, that is, its ability to set the boundaries of any conversation about how things are and what can be done about them, is all but overwhelming; you simply cannot get away from it.

What interests me, however, is the fact that there seems to be no alternative approach to the opposition always put forward here of the subjective versus objective point of view, where religious, or any other value language is relegated to the subjective, while those things promoting an increase in power are always taken as objective. I would like to discuss this opposition as a possible point of entry into whether or not religious language has any role, beyond the expression of opinion, in discussions about the character of communal action, and

I would like to do this against the backdrop of the State's role in serving as the arbiter of what is to be thought real.

The State As Mortal God (Redefining the Problem of Order)

Three years after the Treaty of Westphalia in 1651, a remarkable book was published (interestingly enough, in English), a book that still has the capacity to shock and delight at the same time. It must have been a remarkable era because our political philosophers before and since that book have been much more circumspect in their deliberations and clearly more cautious. Allow me to put before you a selection from the book's preface and let us look at it for a moment, keeping in mind that this is 1651, an era where religion is a central and basic issue, on which men and women staked a great deal – not only their prospects for future life, but also their day-to-day prosperity. It makes the announcement that is, I think, our core issue:

> Nature (the art whereby God hath made and governes the World) is by the *Art* of man, as in many other things, so in this also imitated, that it can make an Artificial Animal. For seeing life is but a motion of Limbs, the beginning whereof is in some principal part within; why may we not say, that all Automata (Engines that move themselves by springs and wheeles as doth a watch) have an artificial life? For what is the *Heart*, but a Spring; and the *Nerves*, but so many *Strings*; and the *Joynts*, but so many Wheeles, giving motion to the whole Body, such as was intended by the Artificer? *Art* goes yet further, imitating that Rationall and most excellent worke of Nature, *Man*. For by Art is created that great Leviathan called a Common-wealth, or State. (in latine Civitas) which is but an Artificiall Man; though of greater stature and strength than the Naturall, for whose protection and defence it was intended; and in which, the Soveraignty, is an Artificall *Soul*, as giving life and motion to the whole body: The *Magistrates*, and other *Officers of Judicature and Execution,* artificiall *Joynts; Reward and Punishment* (by which fastned to the seate of the Soveraignty, every joynt and member is moved to performe his duty) are the *Nerves* that do the same in the Body Naturall; The *Wealth* and *Riches* of all the

particular members, are the *Strength; Salus Populi* (the *peoples safety*) its *Businesse; Counsellors,* by whom all things needfull for it to know, are suggested unto it, are the *Memory; Equity* and *Lawes,* an artificiall *Reason* and *Will; Concord, Health; Sedition, Sicknesse;* and *Civil war, Death.* Lastly, the *Pacts* and *Covenants,* by which the parts of this Body Politique were at first made, set together, and united, resemble that *Fiat,* or the *Let us make man,* pronounced by God in the Creation.

To describe the Nature of this Artificiall man, I will consider

First, the *Matter* thereof, and the *Artificer;* both which is *Man.*
Secondly, *How,* and by what *Covenants* it is made; what are
The *Rights* and just *Power* or *Authority* of a *Soveraigne;* and
what it is that *preserveth* and *dissolveth* it.
Thirdly, what is a *Christian Common-wealth.*
Lastly, what is the *Kingdome of Darkness.*

Concerning the first, there is a saying much usurped of late, That *Wisedome* is acquired, not by reading of *Books,* but of *Men.* Consequently whereunto, those persons, that for the most part can give no other proof of being wise, take great delight to show what they think they have read in men, by uncharitable censures of one another behind their backs.

Notice three things: firstly, the state is artificial, it is a human creation; secondly, it is a machine built on the analogy of the human being, which is to be employed for the benefit and prosperity of those building it, ourselves; and, finally, the author, Thomas Hobbes, tells us, without equivocation, 'lastly, the pacts and covenants, by which the parts of the body politic were at first made, set together and united, resemble that fiat, or "let us make man", pronounced by God in creation.'

Amazing, isn't it? Creating a State is analogous to the act of creation. Herein I think is the point so often disguised by the palliatives of constitutionalism. Hobbes has let it slip that once a State is brought into being, paralleling the act of creation itself, there will now be nothing, in theory, that cannot be accomplished. If the State is an artificial man-made thing, then its actions will be constrained only by artificial boundaries; anything becomes possible in an artificial world, with future possibility reduced essentially and simply to technique and possession of sufficient resources. Reason in this setting becomes instrumental, that is, oriented towards means, and attention is directed to the will, namely what it is that the community desires collectively. Hobbes has let the genie out of the bottle, and in my view he has captured simply and straightforwardly the essential idea underlying the core institutuion of the modern era. Subsequent political theorising has always been a reaction to Hobbes, and again in my view, despite all the ink that has been spilled trying in some way to mitigate the impact of Hobbes's great idea, the reality still remains that the State is the central institution, it defines our era, it is an artificial creation and presumably there is nothing in theory that it cannot do.

What then has made the State possible? How did the state gain such enormous power and capacity? What have been the conditions leading to its centrality? Here I ask not so much what have been the historical conditions; in a nutshell, these can be reduced to war. The mutual and reciprocal effects of providing for defense leading to the need for more defense have given us the incentives to develop our science and administrative capacities. The more intriguing issue is what has changed intellectually. Here I think Hobbes provides the answer once again. For Hobbes, the world, at its basis, is a 'heap'. There is, for the most part, no inherent order in the character of things. Reality, society, the very character of language itself, is essentially arbitrary; when there is order it is imposed from the outside. Hobbes is fairly clear about this. Political order requires a sovereign, a kind of ultimate giver of names who, in establishing these names, defines the boundaries for appropriate collective activity. There has been a lot of scholarly conversation about this proposition. Hobbes, like anyone else working out the consequences of new ideas, can be taken at any point during this process to be saying many different things. However, I think at the core, this is what Hobbes means: political order is artificial, orginating from a single source, the sovereign. Political order must be artificial because there is no inherent order in the nature of things. This is the secret of the State's power. It is, by Hobbes's account, the final artifice, and what makes this claim a real possibility is the less expressed, but nonetheless very real, point that if this order was not present, there would be precious little, if any, order of any kind at all.

Evaluating the Character of Order

The argument to this point comes to this: Hobbes is the point of origin for the phenomenon of practical atheism. Religious language is subordinate to political, i.e., power language becomes political language, which encompasses more. Religous language is presumed to be specific to a given group, subjective, if you will. Political language, on the other hand, is more general, more objective, acting as it does to incorporate as well as accommodate *all* local views in the effort to reconcile the differences that local languages generate. At the foundation of this activity is the view that such order is and must be regnant, for in its absence there would be little to no order at all. The Hobbesian project thus justifies itself very straightforwardly: in the absence of the constructed order there will ultimately be no order. That is the claim for better or worse. Typically, it is always made with provisions in place for some sort of self-restraint. Be that as it may, the central point remains: the ultimate source of order is the State, acting on behalf of the whole, and the order that appears will be a constructed one.

The question now is, how do you evaluate this claim? One might ask, have the goods been delivered? The obvious response, at the present time is, clearly they have. The next question would be, what might we expect? More of the same; that would surely seem to be the case, to paraphrase a famous remark made while admiring one of the earlier works of human ingenuity. 'There seems to be no limit to what they (humankind) can do.' It is hard to come to grips with the evidence of one's senses, which in turn renders any conversation about future possibilities a mute one at best. Out of the artificial order have come safety, abundance and the promise of yet more. Given the requisite administrative technique, sufficient resources, and clear intent, there is nothing that cannot be done. Clearly, one may fairly ask, what is the problem here? Let us accept the terms as they have been given to us, namely, what techniques must we employ, what resources are available, and simply get on with the job.

By way of comparison to this idea, what I now have to say may seem at once too abstract and at the same time instantly obvious. But bear with me. Be again reminded, it is the claim of the Hobbesian State that what is real is, at its foundation, a matter of construction, and thus a question of power and its efficient deployment. I wonder if this claim can be made good? What do I mean? At the limit, which admittedly is still far away, can a sovereign construct a coherent order out of a world that is simply a heap, that is lacking in any inherent order at all? The operative term here is *coherent*. The promise of a constructed order is that it is, in fact, an order where its parts fit together and act in concord. This would seem to be the minimum necessary for establishing the Hobbesian claim, namely that the artificial order will be coherent. We can be assured, in other words, that a blueprint for the constructed order is available and workable. Be reminded that we are speaking at the limit; to show the failures of State action in reality is not the argument, what we want to know in general is, can a coherent order be constructed out of a heap of things, out of a world in which there is no inherent order? It seems to me that if the answer is no, then the State's claim becomes one among many others competing for our attention. The State loses its generality and its power to reduce all other claims to matters of opinion. If the constructed order can only be local, and not general, it too becomes merely a matter of temporary conjunction of technique and resources. If a constructed order is not coherent, in other words, then it cannot be universal, and if it is not universal then its demands for our allegiance have nothing to rest upon other than temporary success.

Let us now evaluate the claim that a coherent order may be constructed out of a collection of unordered things. One way to visualise this problem is to imagine the sovereign or the creator of the order as a calculator, seeking out a solution for an array of equations in which various relations have been stipulated, the objects being described as discrete, that is, represented only by integers and with no connections among themselves other than those stipulated by the sovereign calculator, who is free to choose how the relations are to be set up. It is his world and he can construct it in any way he wants. Now the question of coherence would focus upon whether a universal solution to these types of equations would be possible. The issue of a coherent order is turned into a question of how general can the solution to such equations be? It is known that no universal solution is available for such equations, a remarkable result deriving essentially from the fact that the elements are discrete and there are an infinite number of them. Thus, if the sovereign as a constructor of artificical order is primarily a calculator computing the outcomes of various combinations of discrete unrelated parts, i.e., building up an order, there is no assurance other than a local result that the order is coherent in any final sense. The Hobbesian project is therefore incomplete at its core, there is no guarantee at the formal level that a coherent order can be built up in any general way even given an unlimited supply of computing power.

This seems obvious on the ground level. Practically speaking, we do not seek out general solutions, but work to attain local results with the hope that in the long run the impact will not be too pernicious. But that, it seems, is the core point – Hobbes's claim is that the State reconciles the impact of local orders upon the whole, it is more general, and the more general this reconciliation becomes the less important the local becomes. We are given to believe that it is a matter of technique and resources – better technique, more resources, more order, and the greater level of whatever is being sought. Yet if the image of the sovereign as calculator is taken as a reasonable extension of the metaphor in Hobbes's prefaces, there is no assurance that such a constructed order can be any more coherent by virtue of an increase in technique or resources. The State's claims from this perspective cannot be any more universal than any other. The buck does not, as it were, stop with the sovereign. That voice, contrary to Hobbes's claim, is one among many – a strong one to say the least – but not the only one.

Practical Atheism and the Problem of Order

What do these abstract considerations have to do with the Celtic tiger? Three things. First, if Hobbes is right, then practical atheism will appear, and intensify. Religion will be reduced to the status of opinion, religious diversity will increase, and the emerging social differences will come to parallel religious differences. Second, a secular ethic oriented to the imperatives of politics and market will displace the older ethic grounded on religion and place. Public opinion leaders will promote the trend and take every opportunity to diminish and undermine the older views. Finally, all 'realistic' social action will progressively be directed toward including government, in the effort to satisfy needs. Levels and costs of governance will rise as the levels of demand increase. The older way of life will give way and be transformed in a kind of homogeneity supported by a subsidy, increased consumerism, and even higher levels of State coercion. This is the path that has been followed as the Hobbesian quest for order gets underway.

Is there an antidote? I think for the Irish the answer is yes. The Hobbesian project is flawed at its core. No artificial order can be total. There are therefore intellectual tools for resisting the idealogical hegemony that the State always goes after. This does not mean the choice is between market or State. Those two forces are inextricably linked. To opt for more market and less State, in fact, has always led to more State even in the short run. The crucial point is cost of information. Both states and markets are ways of processing information, which is why they are so closely connected. The new technology that is fuelling the boom here is revealing that the costs of information have been dramatically reduced and will continue to be so. This is the key to beating the Hobbesian dynamic. This empowers the knowledgeable to keep solutions local and avoid the erosion of the more natural community order that the Hobbesian dynamic acts to destroy.

A population armed with intellectual tools for resisting the idealogical demands of the State, combined with a population trained to benefit themselves from the new economic tools is in a great position to develop liveable and viable solutions to the issue of practical atheism and the problem of order. In his recent book, *How the Irish Saved Civilization,* Thomas Cahill showed how Irish monks, the dot.com masters of the era, preserved the cultural history of the West by saving the books. I think it is possible for the same thing to happen now.

SOCIAL JUSTICE AND EQUALITY IN IRELAND

Kathleen Lynch

At this time in history, Ireland, North and South, is facing many new and exciting challenges, challenges that can only be addressed by the development of new ideas, new ways of seeing the world.

Positive political developments in Ireland have been paralleled by profound changes in the global economic and political order. The most visible change has been the advance of sophisticated communications technologies, which has made the local global and the global local. The advance of global communications has been both a product and agent of the growing power and influence of multinational capital. A very small number of transnational corporations either own or control vast amounts of the world's wealth, including the wealth of the communications industry. The interests of global capital, aided and abetted by the powerful nationalist interests of powerful capitalist states, dictate the progress of the global economy, at the expense of millions who live in dire poverty in the marginal economies of the world. Terms of trade, including those within the EU, are set against the interests of many of the poorest peoples of the world. People give aid, but what countries need is fair terms of trade.

To create new social institutions and new political structures that will ensure that global economic developments serve the interests of those without capital, it is imperative that we invest time and energy in developing new ideas about society and its social and political institutions. To create change in society places the same intellectual and resource demands on us as does the creation of a new product in industry. When a company wants to create a new product, it generally invests large sums of money in researching the product, in piloting it, in marketing it, etc. The creation of successful new products is an expensive business. The creation of a new idea about our society, how to organise it economically, socially, politically, is also an expensive business. It takes time to develop new ideas, it takes resources but it also takes a supportive environment. To date, Irish political culture has not been especially supportive of new ideas. Yet we need new ideas, we need to encourage intellectual debate about ideas; to do this means that we need to overcome the profound anti-intellectualism of our political culture. And we also need to overcome the sense of fatalism that is created by political cynicism and detachment. We can change the world, we are the makers of history.

I want to comment therefore on some of the barriers that we need to overcome to allow new ideas to begin to emerge, to allow a supportive environment for change to develop. At this moment in Ireland, there are a number of powerful political ideologies (systems of ideas) that have made it very difficult to realise change, ideologies that need to be named if the silence around change is to be broken. My particular concern is about challenging ideas that allow our society to remain socially unjust.

Rise of Neo-Liberal Politics with a Market Rather than a Social View of the Citizen

One of the most serious difficulties facing those who want to address issues of economic inequality in society is that the political context within which the debate can take place has radically changed internationally. The demise of communism in Eastern Europe, in Russia in particular, has seriously challenged the legitimacy of economic equality as a political project. By implication it has also marginalised political concerns about poverty. Those on the New Right even claim that the problems of poverty have effectively been resolved through the market system (Saunders, 1993). Although such a claim is clearly untenable in the light of the continuing and growing economic inequalities in several countries including Ireland (Atksinson et al., 1995; Coates, 1998; Greider, 1997; Nolan and Maitre, 2000), nevertheless it has enormous political credence evidenced by the serious challenges to the welfare state occurring in several countries in Western Europe. A concept of the 'market citizen' has developed at the expense of the 'citizen with social rights' (Hanson, 2000). The *market view* of the citizen is highly individualised and privatised; it is premised on assumptions of possessive individualism (consumerism) as the defining element in social identity. The individual is defined in terms of her purchasing power, without regard to her wider socio-political responsibilities to fellow citizens, or without regard to the reality of her own dependency on others. The idea that citizenship is untenable without a strong redistributive component and social rights has been seriously undermined.

Part of this neo-liberal ideology is the view that all goods and services can be bought on the open market, including services such as education and health. A diminished role for the State is promoted (and by implication the democratic institutions of the State) in both the distribution of goods and services.

This is a very potent and a very problematic view of society. First, it ignores the reality that the State institutions of our society are, for the most part, democratic institutions. While political institutions are in need of radical overhaul, they are nonetheless publicly controlled by democratically elected people. The elected representatives of the State are held to account by the electorate. There is no democratic regulation of market systems other than those imposed by national or international State systems. Because we live in a capitalist society in which the maximisation of profit is the overriding principle governing market relations, it is profoundly foolish to say that we do not need State interventions to regulate the operation of the market itself. Without such regulation, only such services as were profitable would be made available, and only strong market capacities (market maximisers) would be able to avail of certain services. This has already happened in several areas of the law in this country, because it is effectively a privatised service.

The idea of market-driven service provision is especially problematic in areas such as health, education, and transport systems, as each of these areas are basic to the welfare of our society, albeit in different ways. They are public goods required by all members of society regardless of capacity to pay. Without good health one cannot function personally or socially; without good education one cannot gain access to well paid employment; without good public transport those who are outside the market system especially (the old, the sick, the seriously disabled and the young) simply cannot participate fully as democratic citizens. They are disenfranchised by their immobility. The United Kingdom moved towards market-driven health, transport and education provision during the seventeen years of Thatcher rule, with seriously damaging consequences.

The other problem that I see with the emerging market model of the citizen (the American model as opposed to the European model, as some have put it, although I think this is a simplification of the issue) is that it is based on an abstract concept of the human person. The person is defined as a detached, rational, autonomous entity operating to maximise her or his gain on the market. This perspective ignores any given person's social obligations to other members of society, including their obligation to those on whom their ability to function in the market actually depends. It ignores the reality of their own dependency.

The human person is a dependent person; this dependency is highly visible and multifaceted in infancy, becomes less visible as we gain financial independence, and becomes evident again as we become old and/or disabled. For some, dependency is a lifetime state in terms of their financial or related needs. Both in the case of the individual, and in the case of society as a whole, therefore, dependency on others (and by implication, obligation to others) is part of the normal state of human existence. We may be rational, and at times, autonomous, but we are also living in a state of interdependence. Thus, if we are to have good health services for all those who *need* them as opposed to those with the market capacity *to pay* for them, those of us with market capacities must support those without (children, old people, etc.). The most visible way in which we can do this is through an equitable taxation system. Our obligations arising from dependency are not simply economic, however, they also relate to our emotional and care obligations. As citizens in a community, we have a duty of care, a duty that arises from the profound human need for love, care and solidarity. It is also a duty that arises in recognition of our past, present and likely future dependence on the care of others.

A second area in which neo-liberal thinking has taken hold is in the debate about equality itself. Within the neo-liberal tradition, equality is generally defined in terms of the provision of equal rights to participate in economic, social, political and cultural life, where such rights are construed as the absence of legal and institutionalised barriers to entry and participation in a given institution or system. The belief is that advancement within such institutions and systems should be based on merit. The liberal view of equality also adheres to the principle of non-discrimination in relation to access to, and participation in, public and private services.

While non-discrimination provisions are the legal floor without which equality housing cannot be built, there are serious limits to what such provisions can achieve. At best they can prohibit the grosser forms of discrimination. Indeed, all too often, gross discrimination can continue until a given party takes a case through the courts, and here one is again dependent on the actions of a given individual. Many of those against whom discrimination continues to be practised have neither the emotional nor the financial resources to vindicate their rights.[1]

Even when the equality debate in Ireland moves beyond non-discrimination, much of the concern is about distributing inequalities fairly across social groups, not eliminating the hierarchies of wealth, income, power and privilege that stratify our society in the first instance. It is about remedial rather than radical measures, or what Fraser (1995, 1997) has termed affirmative as opposed to transformative strategies. That is to say, at best there is an argument for equality of participation or outcome for various target groups, where equal outcomes are measured in terms of a *proportionality test*. Equality is deemed to have been attained when the proportion of a given marginalised group attaining privileges (such as the proportion of working class students in higher education, or the proportion of disabled people in employment, or the proportion of women attaining senior management positions) rises relative to their prior rate of participation or success. Inequality is seen to be reduced if the relativities change.

A number of problems are posed by this model of equality. To begin with it acutally reinforces deep forms of inequality by accepting institutionalised structural inequalities in terms of wealth, income, privilege and power (Baker, 1987). The hierarchies remain, so inequalities have to be constantly re-addressed from year to year and generation to generation. Low pay, poor housing, inadequate health and education services remain a problem; all that happens is that, proportionately-speaking, the gender, marital status or social class background of those in élite or subordinate positions may change. Inequalities are distributed differently but the structural injustices persist.

To summarise, what I am suggesting here is that neo-liberalism is a highly problematic political ideology. It has been imported here, largely from the UK and the US, in recent years, with little discussion or debate. It has been proclaimed without being explained. I think it is a political ideology that is anti-democratic, insofar as it places the market rather than the democratic institutions of the State at the centre of policy making. It also ignores the fact that certain goods and services should not be market driven, so fundamental are they to the general good of society; this is true not only of services such as health, education and transport, but also of other services such as those of the law. (After all, it is of little use having laws vindicating your rights, if you are unable to activate these rights to the full, due to inadequate resources). Neo-liberalism is also premised on a detached concept of the individual that does not recognise either the universality of human interdependence or the obligations of interdependence, be that in the area of taxation or the area of care.

One of the reasons why the ideology of neo-liberalism is so problematic is because it is being concealed by a system of consensus politics.

Consensualism, Discourses of Neutrality: Politics Turned in on Itself

At present there is remarkably little public debate about the extent and nature of social inequality and injustice in our society. Political parties seem to be increasingly focused on their own survival, often with very little mention of the values or principles that underpin their politics. It has become increasingly politically fashionable to claim that one has no politics at all (in a recent political debate on television, a member of a large political party in the State stated that the politics of the party in question was to get power), and/or that one's party or group represents all interests equally. This is both politically impossible and empirically unfounded when one reviews the outcomes of the policies enacted by the major parties of this State over many years.

There has been a deepening *consensualisation* governing political discourse, which has led to a serious impoverishment of public debate and a neglect of those who are most marginalised in society. The partnership system, while it has many benefits, has reinforced consensus politics, so that real division of interests between workers and employers, between rich and poor, between women and men, have been suppressed (Allen, 1999). Consensus politics has led to the inevitable dominance of the interests of the more powerful membership of the 'partnerships', as the latter have the resources, systems of influence and capacities to make their expectations and demands the core consensus demands. The interests of the powerful have become 'common sense' interests.

Why did the public allow this to happen? I would suggest that ideology plays a central role in this process of acceptance. By this I mean that powerful ideological formation institutions in the media in particular, but also in other educational and public contexts, such as the Churches, allowed this to happen and actively encouraged consensus at times. For example, consensus politics has been part of Catholic social teaching on resolving issues of class conflict over many decades. The Church encouraged the formation of institutions and systems in society that would create a *via media* between rich and poor, and thereby forestall the development of left/right politics in society. While many of these developments such as that of the promotion of voluntary institutions in civil society (co-operatives, community groups, etc.) are important developments in their own right, nonetheless, they can conceal very real conflicts of interests between groups who are partners to the process.

In more recent times, there have been attempts to suppress feminist ideas and feminist discourses. Women who reject the traditional views of women as the 'exclusive home worker' have also been marginalised and discredited. Feminists have been demonised, presented as men-hating, bitter persons (we have numerous examples of this recently in the media). Yet most feminists are idealists who want to create a new type of society, an inclusive society in which all people will be equal. There is no strand of feminism that proclaims that women are superior to men, although all claim that women are equal to men.

The rejection of difference in political debate has led to a *neutralisation of political discourse*. A discourse/language of classlessness (or sameness) has become normalised in political debate. There is a growing tendency to suggest that Ireland has passed over the class (economic) divide (indeed some claim it never existed), yet economic marginalisation remains the lot of several hundred thousand people. Not only does the 'declassing' of public discourse preclude any serious analysis or public debate about income and wealth inequalities in our society, it also forecloses debates about other interfacing inequalities, such as those relating to disability, women, children, etc. The silencing of debates about economic injustice leads to the development of a culture in which debates about other social injustices can also be trivialised.

The claim to neutrality serves the interests of dominant groups in society as it papers over the deep cracks that divide rich and poor. It effectively delegitimises public debate about social inequality; those who attempt to raise issues of social justice are accused of unearthing the divisions of another age, of trying to break social solidarity or of pursuing self interests by making careers out of poverty. The debate becomes trivialised and diverted into personality battles.

My argument here is that political neutrality and consensualism are often thinly disguised masks for the perpetuation of inequality and injustice. They allow the body public to inhabit a fantasy world in which all people are the same, in which social justice has been achieved, in which there are no divisions except those voluntarily entered into by free choice.

In sum, I am not suggesting that we do not need to co-operate or work closely with other members of society whose views are different to our own. What I am saying it that we need to recognise that oftentimes there cannot and will not be consensus, not least because the interests of those at the negotiating table are directly in conflict with each other. To recognise that there is not consensus is to allow for new political ideas to emerge. Those who dissent from the consensus are no longer defined as cranks, or political misfits, but rather as a valuable part of the body politic that needs to be recognised in terms of its difference.

What Needs to Be Done: A Framework for Creating a More Just and Egalitarian Society: The 3 Rs – Redistribution, Recognition and Representation

To create a truly inclusive and just society, we must develop a holistic approach. We cannot treat one form of inequality, such as educational inequality, independent of economic, social and cultural equality (Baker, 1998). All forms of inequality and social injustice are deeply imbricated with each other. At its most basic, you cannot have equality of opportunity in education without economic, political and cultural equality. Without the latter, the children of privileged parents will always have greater opportunities than the children of the disadvantaged (Shavit and Blossfeld, 1993).

There are three core equality issues that must be addressed in the pursuit of a socially just society. The first of these is the issue of economic equality (fundamentally an issue of the distribution – including ownership and control – and redistribution of primary goods); the second is sociocultural and symbolic equality (fundamentally an issue of the recognition and respect for differences); and the third is political equality (fundamentally an issue of parity in the representation of interests). These equality issues have their origins in distinct forms of injustice that exist in society, namely economic injustices, political and civil injustices, and sociocultural and symbolic injustices.

Economic injustice is rooted in the political-economic structures of our society. It includes various forms of exploitation and deprivation of a material kind. It can take the form of exclusion from employment and wealth ownership, inadequate welfare or income provision, or exploitative pay. *Political or representational injustice* occurs when and where ever power is enacted – for example, in the realms of decision-making, including policy-making, and in political life generally. It may take the form of political exclusion, political marginalisation, political trivialisation or political misrepresentation. *Sociocultural and symbolic injustices* are rooted in patterns of representation, interpretation and communication. They take the form of cultural domination, symbolic misrepresentation or non-recognition all leading to a lack of respect.

All of these forms of equality are closely inter-related. If one dimension of equality is ignored, this can and does have the effect of undermining other equality objectives. The pursuit of a truly inclusive society must a) take account of all three dimensions of the equality project and, b) pursue a radical transformative rather than a liberal remedial approach to inequality.

What is required is the deconstruction of the current economic, sociocultural and political structures of our society leading to a radical transformation. What I mean by this is that the focus of change has to be on social structures and institutions, including the structure of our political, economic, social and cultural institutions. It is not about making minor modifications at the edges of the political and economic system.

What are cultural injustices? Basically they are injustices rooted in patterns of representation, interpretation and communication. They take the form of cultural domination, symbolic misrepresentation or non-recognition, all leading to a lack of respect. Addressing these injustices demands a shift from the politics of tolerance[2] to a politics of recognition that respects and celebrates diversity. It requires an end to cultural imperialism whereby dominant groups in society project their own values and mores as representative of humanity as such. It requires a change from a situation in which ethnic, religious, linguistic or other minorities find their lifestyles and values are either made invisible in public discourse or, if visible, are represented stereotypically or even denigrated (Young, 1990: 58-60). Such a move demands that dominant groups in society critically evaluate their own norms, values and practices. The culture of the dominant is subjected to appraisal, not just the lifestyles and values of the excluded. As the exercise of dominance is often itself an integral element in the identity of powerful groups (Connell, 1995 claims, for example, that dominance is a core element in the definition of masculinity in most societies, while racial supremacism is an integral part of white identity), exploring the cultural assumptions of dominant groups is essential for promoting equality. This is an especially important issue for subordinate groups, as it is they who are generally subject to analysis and investigation by diverse cultural institutions, including research bodies, welfare institutions and the media. In a culturally egalitarian society, the focus of analysis would be re-balanced to focus on the dominant.

All the major cultural institutions of society have to be reviewed and challenged if this is to happen, including the media, education and the churches. While it is clearly necessary to review the ways in which differences are addressed in culture-specific institutions such as the media and education, the issue arises for most service and goods providers in the public and private sectors.

Political inequality refers to injustices in the exercise of power, i.e., when and where power is enacted. As noted above, it refers to all forms of marginalisation, trivialisation or misrepresenation in the political sphere. It can refer to power inequalities within the home, the work place, or the wider political system.

Addressing political inequality demands more accountable, more diverse and more truly representative systems of political representation. Representative democracy has been shown increasingly to have serious limitations, not only in terms of how it can be seriously undermined by the alliances that develop between political and economic elites, but also in terms of how truly representative and accountable it is in highly diverse, mobile, complex societies (Phillips, 1995). In our own society, for example, political constituencies are drawn up on the basis of regional interests (fundamentally along geographical lines), yet many of the major social and political divisions in our society today are not regionally based, gender and social class differences being the clearest examples. There is no formal mechanism within the present political structures to take specific account of the representation of diversity *within* regions. Moreover, there is no recognition of the serious problems posed by a politics of ideas (although it is now arguable whether we have such a system in Ireland any more) divorced from a politics of presence. It is assumed that through the party system, men can effectively represent women, middle class people can represent the interests of working class people, settled people can represent Travellers, etc. Yet representatives have considerable autonomy at the point of decision-making and that is why it matters both who they are and how they are held accountable. As Phillips (1995: 44) points out: 'when there is a significant under-representation of disadvantaged groups at the point of final decision, this can and does have serious consequences'. Their interests can be easily ignored in the privacy of the Cabinet table. It is only when people are consistently present in the process of working out alternatives that they have much chance of challenging dominant discourses and conventions (Phillips, 1995: 45).[3]

At the very least therefore, we need to develop new institutions and procedures for making our democracy more accountable and more truly representative; a move towards a politics of presence would help effect such a change.

The Importance of Economic Equality: The Implications of the Capitalist Order

While it is necessary to pursue all three major equality agendas simultaneously, for many groups, radical economic equality is the major equality project in Ireland at this time. This is not to deny the importance of cultural recognition and respect for many groups, or the need for new and more effective systems of political representation, rather it is to show how difficult it is to pursue either of these objectives without deep economic equality.

One does not have to be a Marxist to realise that we live in a capitalist society within a capitalist-dominated global order. Whether one agrees with capitalism or not, it is blatantly obvious that capitalism produces huge economic and power inequalities, not only within national states but also between them. Within Ireland there is ample empirical evidence documenting the extent and nature of such economic inequalities. While the grosser forms of poverty are on the decline, economic inequalities, as measured in terms of growing wealth and income differentials, continue to grow (Nolan and Maitre, 2000). That the interests of capital exercise powerful control over economic policy, and thereby contribute to such inequalities, is in little or no doubt. Proof has been provided through the various tribunals of recent years, and by the policy initiatives involving substantial reductions in corporation profit taxation and in capital gains tax. Data provided by the Revenue Commissioners (1998) also shows how inequitable the taxation system is. A sizeable minority (one fifth) of very high income earners (incomes over £250,000) had an average (effective) tax rate of 25% or less in 1994/5. Less than one quarter of those with very high incomes faced an effective tax rate of 40% or more, despite the fact that their nominal (marginal) tax rate was 48%.

Capitalism is neither an economic nor a political inevitable. Even though it is not likely to be disbanded in the short term within Western Europe, nevertheless it can be managed and challenged. Levels of economic inequality within capitalist states vary considerably as is evident when one examines the experiences of Sweden, Germany or Japan compared with the US. The levels of economic inequality in our society can be greatly reduced should the political will be there to do so. Although it is not possible to present a blueprint for change in a short paper of this kind, what is possible is to pose some questions. A most obvious case is the growing income differentials that are developing within the waged/salaried sectors of the economy itself. Why is this allowed to happen? Should there not be some concept of a maximum-minimum income ratio between workers' wages, as has existed in Japan for example? Surely one does not need to earn a salary that is ten or even thirty times that of the average worker, as an incentive? In terms of wealth, why do we know so little about wealth ownership and incomes accruing from unearned wealth? Why are systems of taxation on wealth so ineffective? Whose interests are being served by the lack of information and by ineffectual systems of taxation?

Economic inequalities are dysfunctional both socially and economically. They result in the inefficient use of talents and resources as many people cannot deploy their abilities to maximum effect when socially and economically marginalised. Economic inequality also creates extra costs to the State via welfare, housing and health, and fuels a sense of alienation and detachment from society, leading to a breakdown in social solidarity and political cohesion. A society that is strongly polarised in economic terms is not politically stable.

At a more practical day-to-day level, without economic equality it is frequently impossible for people to vindicate other civil and political rights that may be granted to them constitutionally, or to be effective in the representation of their interests. Our system of legal representation operates along private market principles for the most part (something that surely needs to be challenged – if we can have a public health service and a public education service, why not a proper public legal service?). Public service provision for free legal aid is neither adequately funded nor resourced. It is not in a position therefore to offer a full legal aid service to those who may need it to vindicate their rights. The net effect of this is that those with most resources are those who can best afford to have their rights protected; indeed recent evidence from tribunals indicates that not only can they have their interests protected via the courts, they can have their interests enshrined in law and in constitutional principles. This fact in itself makes a mockery of the whole system of justice. It effectively means that those with sufficient money are above the law.

As G.A. Cohen, Professor of Political Theory at Oxford University, said recently at a lecture in University College, Dublin, on 3 November 2000, wealth is a form of freedom. Without money, it is impossible to be totally free in our society (Cohen, 1995). It is absurd to claim that people can exercise their civil and political liberties to the full in a money economy without money, without strong economic rights.

Why Are These Kinds of Issues Not Being Addressed? Problems Posed by the Intellectual Context of the Debate

Higher education and research play a central role in defining the terms in which the debate about economic and social policy take place in society. Consequently, it is important to analyse the way in which key disciplines analyse the question of inequality and poverty and explore the impact that their thinking has on public policy generally. As time does not permit an extensive analysis of all the disciplines involved, I will comment in particular on economics.

Economics

The discipline of economics is a powerful discourse in public policy-making and is dominated by neo-classicalism. Although there is no homogeneity within the discipline in Ireland or within economics as a whole, there is no powerful alternative to neo-classical thought (such as feminist economics or Marxist economics) operating within Ireland. Consequently, it is almost impossible intellectually for a new paradigm to develop. Put simply, intellectual closure within the discipline of economics means that the debate about equality rarely moves beyond concerns with welfarism. There is no serious intellectual challenge to the operation of the capitalist market or to the unequal outcomes of the gendered division of labour; the focus is never on assessing economic structures in terms of such moral considerations as economic justice, enhancing human relations or preserving the environment for future generations. While individual economists are undoubtedly deeply committed to social justice, the constraints of the dominant paradigm within the discipline are overwhelming, leading to an overriding concern with economic efficiency and growth *per se.*

The lack of attention given to the ethical dimensions of the economic order is far from being an exclusively Irish problem, however. It is an endemic problem within the discipline. Internationally, the core principles of the discipline focus on relations between individuals as autonomous rational (normally male) actors rather than people as group members living in states of deep interdependency. The ethical dimensions of economic relations are thus dispelled from consideration without being subject to empirical analysis.

Like economic behaviour itself, the study of economics has become devalued in the sense that moral values have been expelled from consideration. Conversely, values and norms have become de-rationalised so that they become mere subjective, emotional dispositions, lying beyond the scope of reason. Thus, the (attempted) normative-positive split reflect 'a real subjectivisation and de-rationalisation of values on the one hand, and the devaluation and expulsion of moral questions from matters of the running of economics on the other.' (Sayer, 2000: 87).

To say that the ethical is jettisoned from economic analysis is not to deny the deep personal commitment that many economists have to social justice. Moreover, many economists (especially those in the ESRI) have undertaken valuable research on poverty and economic inequality, analysing the ways in which groups and individuals differ in their command over goods and services. Others, including Sen (1987, 1992, 1997) and Roemer (1994) have introduced ethical and critical concepts into economic debates. However, the problem remains that the dominant discourse in economics assumes a positivist split between fact and value, a practice that characterises much sociological analysis of inequality as well (Lynch, 2000).

Economic inequality and poverty are not morally neutral subjects, and their study requires a level of moral engagement that may well not be salient for other issues. To discount the ethical implications of poverty and economic inequality in intellectual analysis, however, is to discount a substantive defining element of the research subject itself. Poverty causes intense and prolonged human misery, especially where it persists over time. To analyse it without regard for its degrading, exclusionary and often life-threatening implications is to ignore a substantive part of what poverty is. It is to confine oneself to a partial analysis of the research subject.

The Gender Order, the Ability Order, the Racial Order, the Age Order, the Sexuality Order . . .

Although I have focused attention in this part of the paper on the economic order in particular, this is not to suggest that there are not other serious social orders in our society that are equally potent in the production of inequality. Although time and space will not allow me to address all of these, the ability order, the racial order, the age order, the sexuality order, etc., I think it is at least important to note their existence. I will, however, comment briefly on the gender order as, next to the economic order, this is arguably the most significant, given its scope and intensity. Moreover, there is an increasingly close correlation between economic inequality and gender inequality; while women are entering employment in ever larger numbers, women as a group are becoming disproportionately represented among the poor, dominating both the welfare classes and the dependent classes in society (Nolan and Watson, 1999).

We live in a society that, like most others societies in the world, is profoundly patriarchal (O'Connor, 1998). That is to say, it is a society in which men are in control of most of the wealth, most of the major institutions of power and decision-making and most of the institutions of cultural production, be these the media, education or the churches. Some simple statistics tell a lot: some 95% of farm owners are men; over 85% of employers are men; 88% of our public representatives are men. The gender order in our society also assumes that *ceteris paribus* (all other things being equal) the feminine is inferior to the masculine, that the work that (mostly) women do in the private sphere (caring in particular) is less valuable than the work that men do in the public sphere. Even within the public sphere, women's jobs have traditionally been defined as being of less value than men's. The net outcome of this is that women are increasingly living in poverty; gender inequality is not simply a cultural problem.

Given the level of control that men exercise over the public life in our society, it is inevitable that our public institutions are organised around the values and interests of powerful men. I think this is a very important point to note; it is the interests of *dominant men* that are enshrined in the cultural codes of our workplaces, in political life, in the churches, etc. Masculinity is plural rather than singular and not all men exercise control and power in society. In his analysis of *Masculinities* (1995), Robert Connell notes that masculinity can be divided into three basic forms or types – *dominant masculinity*, which is exercised by men with money and power; *complicit masculinity*, which operates when relatively subordinate men comply with the values of dominant males in subordinating women and other men, often out of fear, sometimes in the expectation that they too will be dominant some day; and *subordinate masculinity*, which includes men who are gay, men who are from minority cultures, traveller men, black men in white societies, etc.

The failure to recognise the conflict between caring and careers, between caring and capitalist production, for example, can be as much a problem for ordinary men as it is for women. But for men of power and men of money, it is generally not a pressing concern (at least until recently when there is a shortage of labour), as they generally do not have to manage the daily conflicts that arise between caring for others who are dependent on one emotionally and socially, and holding down a job or pursuing a career.

What I am saying, therefore, is that there is a gender order that not only assumes that women are generally subordinate to men, it also assumes that different classes of men are subordinate to other men (and indeed to some classes of women). The significance of this for society is that our public and social institutions frequently ignore the interests of women and subordinated men in their social construction. Family-friendly policies are not a feature of most of our work environments; child-care and care of dependent older people or disabled persons are only minimally supported in our social welfare and employment codes. Most of our public institutions are organised around values and principles that ignore the reality of human interdependency and the need for people to have time to care for others and to be cared for. Gender equality demands that the current gender order is challenged and that the interests of women and most men, not just those of the powerful and influential, define the terms of social and political systems.

Conclusion

At the present time, many of the great achievements of Western civilisation are being threatened by the rise of the New Right – the right to social entitlements such as decent healthcare, welfare and housing, the right to protection and care in old age; the right to a good education for all, not just for those who can pay; the right of the vulnerable to protection from the vicissitudes of a global market economy. Economic monetarism has become a type of religion; increasingly, the only work that is of value is that which can be exchanged for profit. By logical extension, those who are unable to be economically productive or profit generating are deemed valueless; they are degraded and marginalised.

If we are to create a new vision for Ireland, a realisable vision, then we must begin to challenge the ideologies of neo-liberalism, dressed up as it is in the fatalistic clothes of 'globalisation', 'flexible' labour markets, etc. We must not be afraid of intellectual debates and conflicts, or indeed of taking up a new language to name what needs to be done. We must also identify the principles and procedures that will guide our social, economic and political institutions through systematic research, analysis and planning. While life cannot be made to order, the quality of our life can be greatly improved by collaborative work between all of those with an interest in creating a caring, participative and socially just society.

I have argued here as well that there are three core contexts in which we need to work actively to create an egalitarian society, namely the economic context, the political context and the sociocultural context. There are three basic equality principles that need to guide action in each of these if we are to have a socially just society, namely the 3Rs of equality – we need more effective and fairer mechanisms for the *redistribution of wealth;* we need to put operational procedures throughout all our cultural institutions that *recognise and celebrate differences;* and we need to develop systems for the *representation of interests* in power and decision making that are effectively, as opposed to formally, inclusive.

Notes

1. This is not to deny that changes in the law based on the liberal assumption of non-discrimination at the point of access (to a given set of opportunities, institutions or positions) undoubtedly reinforce equality principles in a public and statutory context: they grant non-discrimination principles new authority and status, thereby inspiring changes in social behaviour and attitudes. However, attitudinal and institutional changes are realised very slowly by these mechanisms.

2. Tolerance of its very nature is a hierarchical concept as it implies that there is a person or group tolerating (the powerful and important) and a group or person being tolerated (the powerless and of lesser importance).

3. Indeed, 'There is something distinctly odd about a democracy that accepts a responsibility for redressing disadvantage, but never sees the disadvantaged as the appropriate people to carry this through.' (Phillips, 1995:43–44)

References

Allen, K. 1999. 'The Celtic Tiger, Inequality and Social Partnership.' *Administration*, Vol. 47, No. 2 (1999), 31–55.

Atkinson, A., et al. *Income Distribution in OECD Countries: The Evidence from the Luxembourg Income Study.* Paris: OECD, 1995.

Baker, J. *Arguing for Equality.* New York: Verso, 1987.

Baker, J. 1998. 'Equality.' In *Social Policy in Ireland.* Edited by S. Healy and B. Reynolds. Dublin: Oak Tree Press, 1988.

Blossfeld, H. P., and Y. Shavit. 'Persisting Barriers: Changes in Educational Opportunities in Thirteen Countries.' In *Persistent Inequality.* Edited by S. Shavit and H.P. Blossfeld. Oxford: Westview Press, 1993.

Coates, K. 'Unemployed Europe and the Struggle for Alternatives.' *New Left Review* 227 (1998).

Clancy, P., and J. Wall. *Social Background of Higher Education Entrants.* Dublin: Higher Education Authority, 2000.

Cohen, G.A. *Self Ownership, Freedom and Equality.* Cambridge: Cambridge University Press, 1995.

Cohen, G.A. *If You're an Egalitarian, Why Are You So Rich?* Oxford: Polity Press, 2000.

Combat Poverty Agency. *Disability, Exclusion and Poverty.* Dublin: Combat Poverty Agency, 1994.

———— *Poverty: Lesbians and Gay Men.* Dublin:

Connell, R. W. 1995. *Masculinities.* Cambridge: Polity Press, 1995.

Connelly, A., ed. *Gender and the Law in Ireland.* Dublin: Oak Tree Press, 1993.

Crompton, R. *Class and Stratification.* Polity Press: Cambridge, 1993.

Fraser, N. 'From Redistribution to Recognition? Dilemmas of Justice in a "Post-Socialist" Age.' *New Left Review* 212 (1995), pp. 68–93.

Fraser, N. *Justice Interruptus: Critical Reflections on the 'Postsocialist' Condition.* New York: Routledge, 1997.

Greider, W. *One World, Ready or Not: The Manic Logic of Global Capitalism.* New York: Touchstone, 1997.

Hanson, P. 'European Citizenship: Or Where Neoliberalism Meets Ethno-culturalism.' *European Societies,* Vol. 2, No. 2 (2000), pp. 139–165.

Lynch, K. 'Research and Theory on Equality and Education.' In *Handbook of the Sociology of Education.* Edited by M. Hallinan. New York: Kluwer Academic/Plenum Publishers, 2000.

Nolan, B., and B. Maitre. 'Income Inequality.' In *Bust to Boom: The Irish Experience of Growth and Inequality.* Edited by Brian Nolan et al. Dublin: IPA, 2000.

Nolan, B., and D. Watson. *Women and Poverty.* Dublin: Oak Tree Press, 1999.

O'Connor, P. *Emerging Voices: Women in Contemporary Irish Society.* Dublin: Institute of Public Administration, 1998.

O'Neill, C. *Telling It Like It Is.* Dublin: Combat Poverty Agency, 1992.

Phillips, A. *The Politics of Presence.* Oxford: Oxford University Press, 1995.

Phillips, A. *Which Equalities Matter?* Oxford: Polity Press, 1999.

Revenue Commissioners. *Revenue Commissioners Survey: Effective Rates of Tax for High-Earning Individuals* (Summary of Findings). Dublin: Office of the Revenue Commissioners, 1998.

Roemer, J. *A Future For Socialism.* New York: Verso, 1994.

Saunders, R. 'Citizenship in a Liberal Society.' In *Citizenship and Social Theory.* Edited by B. Turner. London: Sage, 1993.

Sayer, A. 'Moral Economy and Political Economy.' *Studies in Political Economy* 61 (Spring), pp. 79–103, 2000.

Sen, A. *Ethics and Economics.* Oxford: Basil Blackwell, 1987.

———. *Inequality Reexamined* Oxford: Clarendon Press, 1992.

———. *On Economic Inequality.* Oxford: Clarendon Press, 1997.

Shavit, S., and H. P. Blossfeld, eds. *Persistent Inequality.* Oxford: Westview Press, 1993.

Young, I.M. *Justice and the Politics of Difference.* Princeton: Princeton University Press, 1990.

View From the Chair

Kate Ó Dubhchair

Welcome to the Chair begins long before one takes possession of the furniture. It begins when you arrive in Ennis and step into an atmosphere that says 'This is something special!'

The morning of my sojourn started with well-wishes from some new-found friends of the previous night. (There's nothing like a hug to set you up for the day). I was also given some expert advice from a lovely woman from the locality who had impressed me in many ways – not least by the fact that she had opted to stay in the hotel, although home was nearby, so as not to miss anything. And then we were off with Fr Harry, making the introductions. He said it was the short version, but . . . !

Last year I had experienced the period of reflection from the floor. This year it was a great privilege to lead that time and offer a few thoughts on our overall theme of Time and Presence. The thoughtfulness was palpable and seemed to connect us all together in our common search for answers and direction. In two minutes we became a community.

Our morning session was entitled 'How Do We Handle the Next Ten Years?' and the first speaker was Professor Gearóid Ó Tuathaigh, who took a historical perspective. He proposed that we should look at the future through the lens of the past and allow it to be historically sensitised. He offered an optimistic outlook but tempered it with realism. His words reminded me of those of Thomas Moore, who suggested that now and then we need to remember our disabled past rather than our enabling future in order that our progress be grounded in values and have that essential element of mystery.

Despite having promised to look after timekeeping, I exercised the Chair's prerogative and made no attempt to restrain Professor O'Tuathaigh as he finished his prepared text and continued in 'freeflow'. He spoke of the consultative and participatory climate of public policy but asked was it for real or for show. He hoped for a coalition of the theoretical and the practical, and a resultant increased awareness – consciousness in a broken world. This was pure gold and the coffee could wait.

As it transpired, the 'Chair' and speakers had little time for coffee. Instead we tried to pose naturally for the ubiquitous photograph. Our second speaker, Dr Maureen Gaffney, is an old hand at this publicity game and she graciously led the way. I had pleasure in introducing her as a friend, even though this was our first meeting in person. Like many at the conference, I have always enjoyed her writing in *The Irish Times* and particularly her recent renderings in the new Saturday *Irish Times Magazine*.

Professor Ó Tuathaigh had ended his discourse with some comments on social capital and this led neatly into Dr Gaffney's address entitled 'Rebuilding Social Capital: Restoring the Ethic of Care in Irish Society'. She defined social capital in terms of both the values that bind – trust and reciprocity – and the dense web of relationships in our society. I loved her term 'thick values' and the value she placed on the importance of our innate sense of belonging. Dr Gaffney spoke of the many challenges and opportunities facing us in a global world and information society and the potential for the free-flow of information to empower the individual. She spoke of speed and competitiveness and the drive of consumerism. In her opinion we are living off the fat of an earlier Ireland – a large young population, an intense belief in education, and a unique experiment in social partnership.

The lesson and the question were clear: today's prosperity comes to us out of the investment of our predecessors in our future – what is our investment today in our society's future? We are conscious of the pervading existence of the Ethic of Power, how then can we re-introduce an Ethic of Care? A good starting place for a lively discussion. Unfortunately it did not proceed as interactively as one might have hoped. There is always a temptation for delegates to make statements rather than pose questions. While all interjections are valuable, with such large numbers it does pose a problem for the person charged with letting as many speak as possible. From the Chair I registered frantic signalling from Máire Johnston and I resolved to take a firm stance in the afternoon session.

Returning promptly at 2.30 p.m. as directed, we were soon underway again. True to my word, I suggested to all that when we came to question and answer time everyone who wished to speak should confine themselves to two sentences, one of which ideally should end in a question mark. There was a good-humoured response and then we all fell silent again, leaving behind the bustle of lunchtime conversation and focussing in on our continuing theme, 'What Values Shape Modern Society?'

I welcomed to the platform the first of our two speakers from the US, Dr Bill Collins. Dr Collins led us to reflect on the effect of diversity. Ireland, perhaps for the first time, is welcoming significant numbers of people from other shores. In America there is great diversity but, while it provides a rich tapestry, it also throws up new problems. He cautioned us to be aware that with diversity comes change. He seemed to see diversity as sister to disconnectedness and putting these together we actually breed indifference. In a diverse environment much is often delegated to the State. The State, *per se*, deals in generalities and issues of ethics, and politics are thus reduced to matters of personal opinion or local preference. Accepting that diversity is a fact of life, one must then accept responsibility for connecting with one's family, with one's community, with those elected to govern. To do less is to abdicate responsibility.

Dr Collins finished by advocating the need for wisdom, that we might know how to order things. The words of A.W. Small came to mind:

> The institutions which our generation inherits may be very crude . . . he who would re-order them should first understand them.

Fifty years ago people spoke of knowledge and wisdom as values giving one the ability to understand, to predict, to plan and to assess. Have we allowed progress to turn these social and contextual skills into a commodity we call information?

Our final speaker, Dr Kathleen Lynch, rose to the challenge of addressing this and other questions of social justice and equality in Ireland. She urged us to develop a new language that spells out our ideals, to have courage and to encourage debate and intellectual discourse. She castigated the privatisation of knowledge and advocated a knowledge democracy. She spelled out three core principles of social inclusion: redistribution, recognition, and representation. In calling for change in all three areas, Dr Lynch graphically illustrated the degree of hypocrisy in our present systems. In listening I was struck by the extent to which we have 'sloganised' our values and become a society of catch-phrases. As Dr Lynch concluded, we need to challenge the ideologies of neo-liberalism and together create an inclusive, caring and participative society.

As you can imagine, there was no shortage of questions and, in this session, there was genuine co-operation, meaning that more people could interact with the panel. As I bounced balls back and forth to Doctors Lynch and Collins, I marvelled at their mental dexterity, from issues of philosophy to disability, to the environment, to life in our universities. They fielded them all and I brought the afternoon to a close with a feeling of real gratitude to all our speakers and satisfaction with the day's conversation.

But my chairing job was not quite over. The next day I was charged with summarising our thinking and providing a link into Day Two. The academic and philosophic world gave way to the world of commerce and the media. I signed off leaving chair and platform to the ebullient David McWilliams.

Final thoughts on the 'View from the Chair'? First of all I think I got more than I gave and I thank all the speakers. I also want to thank the conference organisers. In more than twenty years of conferences I have never attended one that was more professionally organised or more people-friendly. My chairing was made easy with instructions, notes and real-time hand signals. My congratulations to all the team.

In his introduction, Fr Harry had alluded to the fact that I had spent the year dealing with cancer. This was my first step back into public life. His words evoked a beautiful response from those present. It was humbling for me and I will remember in my prayers so many people who offered me theirs.

On the substance of the debate, the papers speak for themselves. I can only say that I felt totally affirmed in my belief in the necessity of this dialogue. In the words of T. S. Eliot, I am convinced that 'the end of all our exploring will be to arrive where we started and know the place for the first time'.

Day Two

Part One: Economics, As If People Mattered?

Two corporations give examples of practices within their own organisations:
Orla Kelly, Organisational and Effectiveness Manager, Hewlett Packard (Manufacturing) Ltd:
'Diversity Practices at Hewlett Packard'
John Liddy, Managing Director, Roche (Ireland) Ltd:
'Business As a Means, Not an End'

Putting People at the Centre of Things
Robert E. Lane

Part Two: Can Anything Be Permanent in a Changing World?

Why Are We Deaf to the Cry of the Earth?
Seán McDonagh

'It's Just the Media!'
Colum Kenny

View from the Chair
David McWilliams

DIVERSITY PRACTICES AT HEWLETT PACKARD

Orla Kelly

My first encounter with Rural Resource Development was last year when Catherine McGeachy called me and told me that I should attend the conference. I found it very stimulating and I really enjoyed the couple of days. When I was asked to come back this year to talk about company practice, I was delighted to do so.

Today I am not going to talk about economics. 'Do people matter?' – I'm not going to invest too much time in that question; I'm sure we all agree that people do matter. I have thought long and hard about what I would talk about here today. There is a wide range of established practices at Hewlett Packard that I could talk about, but I decided to choose managing diversity, for a number of reasons. Firstly, I did a thesis on that subject a number of years ago and I feel very passionate about it. Secondly, I believe that this is a critical factor that organisations need to take into account in their business strategy and something that really affects competitiveness. Thirdly, I think that it is something that every individual can connect with. There are people here in this audience who are not necessarily working with corporations, who may be in the voluntary sector or the community sector, but I think this whole topic of diversity is one that impacts all of us, both individually and as part of the society in which we live. When I picked the topic I didn't realise how popular it was; almost every speaker so far has mentioned it.

I want to begin with a brief overview of Hewlett Packard (HP) and share with you some information about our corporate objectives and our values. I will then talk about the concept of managing diversity, what it means and the business case for doing it. Finally, I will tell you how Hewlett Packard defines diversity in the workplace and I will look at some of the practical ways in which we at Hewlett Packard have gone about creating an inclusive work environment. There will be some theoretical stuff at the beginning, but hopefully by the end I will get an opportunity to share some practical examples of actual deliverables that we have been able to achieve this year.

Hewlett Packard is a very large high-technology company employing almost 90,000 people worldwide. In Ireland we have had a sales operation since 1977, and then in 1995 it was decided to set up a manufacturing site. HP bought a 200-acre site in Leixlip in County Kildare and built a facility there. Primarily we are involved in the manufacture of Ink Jet Cartridges for our Desk Jet Printers. We employ 1,700 people directly in the manufacturing area, we have over 100 people involved in sales and a number of other businesses on site, so we now have a technology campus rather than a manufacturing facility. To grow from a greenfield site in 1995 to employing more than 2,000 people in 2000 has been quite a challenge. HP has quite a distinct organisational culture and one of our challenges when we set up in Ireland was to ensure that this culture was embedded in the organisation.

HP was founded by two graduate engineers in 1939, Bill Hewlett and Dave Packard. They had a unique approach to management, the 'HP way', which has very much stood the test of time. I would now like to share with you HP's corporate objectives, which were written in 1957. They still remain our objectives today.

1. Profit 'To achieve sufficient profit to finance company growth and to provide the resources we need to achieve our other corporate objectives.' I think that is fairly straightforward. I think the primary objective of every company is profit. HP's approach was to re-invest profit – rather than getting into a situation where it was funding growth through debt, it always had a conservative approach to financing, funding research and development through re-investing profit.

2. Customers. In terms of customers, our objective is 'To provide products and services of the highest quality and of the greatest possible value to our customers, thereby gaining and holding their respect and loyalty.'

3. Fields of Interest. 'To participate in those fields of interest that build upon our technologies, competencies and customer interests, that offer opportunities for continuing growth, and that enable us to make a needed and profitable contribution.' Initially HP was involved in the test and measurement area, it is now very much involved in computing – personal computers and printers.

4. Growth. 'To let our growth be limited only by our profits and our ability to develop and produce innovative products that satisfy real customer needs.' Obviously a healthy organisation needs to grow. There is a strong belief that in order to attract people to an organisation and to retain them, employees needed to be associated with a growing company. That was a priority even back in the 1950s.

5. Our People. This is the objective that, I believe, shows the most foresight, given that it was written in 1957: 'To help HP people share in the company's success, which they make possible; to provide them with employment security based on performance. To create with them an injury-free, pleasant and inclusive work environment that values diversity and recognises individual contributions, and to help them gain a sense of satisfaction and accomplishment from their work.' I think the fact that diversity is mentioned here shows a lot of vision. That is a very fundamental objective, which has always been core to HP in the way that we operate.

6. Management. In terms of management, our objective is 'To foster initiative and creativity by allowing the individual great freedom of action in attaining well-defined objectives.' We have a system of management by objectives, whereby people agree objectives with their managers and then have considerable autonomy and freedom to achieve these.

7. Citizenship. 'To honour our obligations to society by being an economic, intellectual and social asset to each nation and each community in which we operate.' That is an important objective for HP and involves quite a number of projects, such as employment security, contributing to the environment, investing time and resources in community projects, and so on.

These objectives have stood the test of time – they have been in place now for over forty years and they form the backbone of the way we work.

At HP, we have five underlying organisational values that guide us as we work towards our objectives. Added to that, we have values that are guiding principles for the way we work. Firstly, we have trust and respect for individuals. Trust is a very important principle in HP. We believe that everyone wants to do a good job and if they are given the resources and the tools, they will. So there is a high level of trust in employees. It was interesting to hear Maureen Gaffney talking yesterday about the whole issue of trust and how important it is for companies to have that in order to be successful.

Secondly, as an organisation, we focus on a high level of achievement and contribution in order to be a high performing company. People are challenged to contribute and to meet their objectives. Thirdly, we conduct our business with uncompromising integrity and this is aligned with our corporate objective around citizenship. We expect very high standards of integrity and of business conduct in our dealings with suppliers and the community as well as with employees.

Fourthly, we encourage flexibility and innovation, and, lastly, we achieve our common objectives through teamwork. Teamwork is critical to HP. Coming from the top down we have high-level corporate objectives, which then cascade down, so that each individual can relate to the organisational objectives, and we aim to have an environment of co-operation where people can work together to achieve those objectives. We encourage flexibility and innovation so that people are given autonomy and freedom.

These are our five core values. I am not going to stand here today and say that everything at HP is wonderful and that we do everything perfectly, but certainly we do our utmost to live those values and they do come through in the work that we do.

I will now talk about HP's commitment to managing diversity. I think it is very important to look at that in the context of our objectives and our values because they very much fit together. Diversity – what is it? I am sure we all have our opinions on what it is; the textbooks are packed with definitions of it. What I will share with you here today is how HP views it. Something that is of interest to me is that every speaker yesterday talked about it. Five years ago I joined HP and at the time I was doing an MBA. I decided to do my thesis on managing diversity. As part of that I went out and did some research – I spoke to a number of high-profile employers in the country at the time and no one knew what I was talking about; the term diversity simply had not been heard of. I think it is very interesting that in the space of five years it has become such a commonly used term – I think in some cases a misused term, but certainly a commonly used one.

It is accepted generally that managing diversity and that whole topic had its roots in America in the form of affirmative action. However, it has moved a lot further since then. In America in the '70s, affirmative action was very much externally driven. The focus was on meeting legal requirements, meeting quotas, targets, etc. That has changed and now it has become an internally driven conversation. Companies have realised that it is something that they really need to do for their own business success, rather than something that they are being forced to do. That is quite a significant shift. I think that in Ireland we are somewhere between the two. In the US they have probably moved a little further because they started earlier. Ireland has not been through that affirmative action phase. We have had the opportunity to learn a lot from that and to move on.

Companies now have strategic action around diversity; I know that in HP it is regularly discussed at the highest levels in the organisation, and it is very much part of our business strategy. The same is true for many other organisations. I think there has been a movement away from group focus. In the '70s and early '80s the focus was on eliminating discrimination, righting the wrongs of the past and focusing on group membership. The focus is now more on the individual. It looks at individuals' needs rather than the needs of people associated with certain groups. If we look at any group, for example, women, or people with disabilities, we will see that not all people in the group are the same. They have different talents, different educations, different desires, and different abilities. More and more, the focus within organisations has to be around valuing the individual and not necessarily focusing on the group. Group focus can be very useful, but I think it is a very simplistic way of looking at diversity and can sometimes prove rather more exclusive than inclusive. As we move forward and learn more about this topic we will see more of a focus on the individual than on the group, although there are certain cases where there still needs to be a focus on group membership. Our own Employment Equality Act, 1998, does specifically allow for positive action, in respect of particular groups in society based on age, gender, and disability.

We are moving away from seeing diversity as a liability, or something that is to be tolerated, towards a place where diversity is seen as an asset. Again, in the past, diversity was seen as something we had to live with, with people being expected to conform to the organisational culture that they were in, the dominant culture. Employees will no longer accept this. Employees want to be valued for their individuality. They won't accept being expected to conform.

Another interesting fact to note about this topic of diversity is a report that was published in the US, the Hudson Report of 1987, which looked at what was going to affect US demographics and the US labour force from 1987 to the year 2000. The predictions made in that report forced a lot of organisations to rethink the whole diversity situation and helped to move the emphasis away from equal opportunities and preventing discrimination towards really *valuing* people. One prediction was that women would account for 60 per cent of new entrants to the workforce between 1991 and 2000, another was that by the year 2056, whites would be outnumbered by other ethnic groups in the population. I think that we here in Ireland are in a position where we can learn from the experiences of other countries and take it from there.

At HP, diversity is summed up as follows: 'The existence of many unique individuals in the workplace, marketplace and in the community. That includes men and women from many different nations, cultures, ethnic groups, lifestyles, generations, backgrounds, skills and abilities.' That is how we define diversity. We believe that diversity brings many benefits to the organisation. It is not simply about recruiting diversity into the workplace, and I think this is one of the traps that organisations can fall into. It does not necesssarily follow that by recruiting diversity into the workplace they will have a diverse workforce. The environment has to such that people who may be different can be *valued* and *included* in that workplace. So we have a strategy and objectives around inclusion, so that inclusion is the work environment that we are creating, where everyone has the opportunity to fully participate in creating business success and is valued for the distinctive skills, experiences and perspectives that they bring to the workplace. It also describes the global community that we are building as we work to connect everyone and everything through our products, services and our winning workforce.

Think for a moment about someone who is different, who is, for example, homosexual, working in an organisation where that cannot be spoken about, where it is kept quiet. Think about the amount of energy that this person has to use to keep that part of their life hidden, energy that could be put into building relationships in the workplace and contributing to the organisation. Then you see how much energy and how much potential can be lost in organisations. If people can't talk comfortably about who they went on holidays with or what they did at Christmas, . . . well, these are small examples but they are things that we do not take into consideration as much as we should. The environment we are trying to create is one where it is okay to be different, where in fact people are valued for their difference. It is a difficult task and I think it is a journey that we are going to be on for a very long time. I am not sure if any organisation is going to be able to sit back on its laurels and say that they are totally inclusive and that everything is wonderful, but certainly that is what we aspire to. I think organisations need to give some thought as to how they can create that kind of environment. I will talk to you a little later on about some of the things that we have done to that end.

I am not going to go into the dimensions of diversity in detail but you will notice that there are visible ways in which people are different and there are also invisible ways. Age and gender are perfectly obvious ways in which you can see someone as different from yourself. On the other hand, thinking styles is certainly an invisible one. So we need to look at the obvious and the less obvious ways in which people are different. These are our dimensions as we use them in HP. There is a huge amount of literature that would go much further than that, looking at a whole range of differences, from those that are very core to the individual, to those that are only related to the work that they are involved in, but this is how we define it. It is interesting in some of the work that we do, in some of our workshops with our employees, that when you ask people to list the dimensions of diversity, you could end up with a list of sixty, ranging from tastes in music to dress – it can really go to any extreme.

Now I would like to look at valuing diversity from a business perspective. I am only going to touch on this topic because there is so much research out there that I cannot possibly do it justice here today.

I think most people can relate, on an intellectual level, to why diversity and valuing it in the workplace is important or why socially or ethically it is important that people are not discriminated against, but a lot of people may not clearly see the business case for that. I am going to share some of the reasons why we need to look at that.

One reason is labour supply. We all know that we are working in a far tighter labour market than we had ten years ago. The demographics of that market force have changed. Organisations need to hire the best person for the job. They need to explore sources of that talent. Ten years ago you did not see organisations going overseas to take part in recruitment fairs. The whole area of recruitment is a key one; we are seeing people look for different sources of talent. I think there is a huge amount for us to learn about how this takes place – you heard Maureen Gaffney talk yesterday about people retreating to be with like-minded people, well, that can be a tendency in the workplace also. There has been a lot of research done about recruitment and how interviewers tend unconsciously to recruit people who are like themselves – people with whom they can possibly establish a rapport quickly. That is not necessarily in the organisation's best interests.

From a retention point of view, our marketplace is such that people have a choice as to where they want to work. An organisation needs to meet the needs of the employee, which are different now than they were in the past. People expect to be recognised for their contribution. They are no longer satisfied with a salary; they want a lot more – they want a satisfying work life, they want something that is fulfilling, they want career development opportunities. Again these must be tailored to the individual. An organisation needs to take into account that all types of people can be successful. Research in the US shows that graduates, when considering a job offer now, will take into account whether the company has a policy on diversity. They will look to see if there is a role model, someone like them, on the management team. That is certainly something that wasn't seen ten years ago. We haven't reached that stage in Ireland yet, but I think it's only a matter of time, because people now have that choice.

People are also expecting a level of work/life harmony from their employers. We use this term in HP instead of balance because we have a belief that people really want to harmonise their life rather than just balance it. It is not an 'either/or' choice; it is both life and work, they are both very strongly connected for most people. There will be times when your life intrudes on your work and there will be times when your work intrudes on your life. What we try is to do is offer flexibility that allows people the ability to harmonise the two. We have done quite a lot of work in this area. I am not going to go into it today but it is closely aligned with the diversity question. We also need to take into account the changing needs of family. We have seen that family structures have changed. Organisations need to be flexible to meet those needs.

Then there is team effectiveness. There is a great deal of research that shows that diverse teams are more effective than homogeneous teams. They may take longer to get up and running, because there may be more time invested up front in terms of establishing relationships and understanding communication styles, but ultimately it has been proven that heterogeneous or diverse teams often out-perform homogeneous teams when performing complex tasks. HP is a very strong engineering company. Often we find ourselves among a number of engineers who all seem to have the same approach to tackling a problem. However, if someone from finance goes in there, they may have a completely different way of approaching the same task. That's one of the benefits that diversity can bring to a team. It also brings a higher level of innovation and creativity because again you are tapping into different perspectives, different ideas, and that can be very valuable.

Those are some of the major business reasons for valuing diversity. We do believe that diversity is critical to our business success for many other reasons, which I do not have time to go into today. We believe that diversity in an organisation leads to creativity. Creativity generates invention. Our organisation began as a partnership of two inventors and we need to continually invent new products, new services. The Internet world is very fast-paced and we need to be at the cutting edge, so invention is very important to us. Invention will drive profitability and business success. That, in turn, will help us to achieve our company vision. So we have to continue to be a competitive company, to be a winning company, but also to maintain a culture that values people in everything we do. For work on diversity to be successful, an organisation has to have a vision, a vision of where it wants to go. In HP we have that vision. There also has to be a commitment from the leadership in the organisation. Working on diversity can be a very thankless task, because what you are doing all the time is working on people to challenge their beliefs about the world and how it works. We all have baggage, from things that happened in our lives, from the stereotypes that we have been brought up with, and diversity work often involves challenging that.

What I would now like to give you are some practical examples of what we have done to value diversity at HP. Each year we develop a plan around how we are going to progress our diversity strategy in Ireland and our inclusion plan for that year. In 1995, when we started here, we immediately focused on recruitment. We ran a number of programmes, for example, to promote age diversity in the workplace – bringing long-term unemployed back into the workplace, to encourage women to return to work. Our focus now continues to be on these areas but has widened to include a number of others. Behind our plan for the year 2000 was a series of deliverables and project plans, which I haven't time to go into in detail, but basically what we set out to do this year was to focus on nine different areas. The first of these areas is leadership development. Leadership is very critical for any organisation that wants to make progress on this topic. In HP this comes from the very top, from our CEO. In Ireland our senior management team are also committed to it and we have done a huge amount of development work with them. Every two months I facilitate a development workshop around diversity with them. Again they recognise that this is an area where the more you learn, the more you realise you didn't know. I believe that we are a very pro-active organisation in this regard, but we still recognise that with an organisation of our size there may be challenges. There may be occasions when our behaviour falls far below what we might like it to be.

We do have a policy against harassment and bullying and, as part of that, this year we put in place a formal structure for investigating complaints. We also put in an informal structure where we trained a number of employees, at all levels and across all functions in the organisation, in employment equality legislation, including harassment and bullying and what it means, and they are now informal contact people who will help employees to deal with issues when they arise. We all know that when an issue like this arises, the easiest and best way is to resolve it locally.

We also revised our equal opportunities policy, to reflect the new employment equality legislation. In terms of management development we continue to work with that group to develop them. This year they received disability awareness training, awareness training on the employment equality legislation, and so on. Awareness training for employees was a big initiative this year. It is one thing to educate management, but our employees are crucial. We developed a workshop where we get employees together for half a day to explore what diversity means, what inclusion in the workplace means, what exclusion looks like. We ask people to think of practical examples of when they have seen exclusion happen in our organisation. We receive very good feedback on it. Again it gives people the opportunity to explore things that they may not otherwise explore. While we do diversity and awareness training in our new employee induction, we felt that it was important to make it an ongoing thing. This year, more than three hundred of our employees have gone through these workshops.

In the area of disability we felt that we needed to make some progress so we applied for the Positive to Disability Award, in which we were successful. We have also put in place a programme where we have a group of managers working to see what we can do to be more positive to disability. We have been working with outside agencies in terms of placing people with disabilities. We have also done a lot of awareness raising around this. We are not there yet but we are working on it.

In terms of accountability we have to find exactly what we expect from our managers – again it is one thing putting in place a strategy like this, but if people are not held accountable, nothing will happen, so we hold people accountable for it. We have feedback mechanisms, such as a regular employee survey, which measures employee satisfaction and also look at inclusiveness in the workplace, how people feel valued. We find this to be a good measure. We also do interviews with employees where we explore these issues. When someone leaves they have a one-hour meeting with a HR person to get feedback on a whole range of issues, including diversity.

The last area of activity for 2000 is around indicators. We don't have measures, we don't have quotas around diversity, but we do track indicators. We look at our hiring profile, take up of flexible work options, etc.

My final thought. This is a quote that I think is very useful. It is from Roosevelt Thomas, Jr, and it appeared in the *Harvard Business Review,* March–April 1990:

> Think of corporate management for a moment as an engine burning pure gasoline. What's now going into the tank is no longer just gas, it has an increasing percentage of, let's say, methanol. In the beginning, the engine will still work pretty well, but by and by it will start to sputter, and eventually it will stall. Unless we rebuild the engine, it will no longer burn the fuel we're feeding it. As the work force grows more and more diverse at the intake level, the talent pool we have to draw on for supervision and management will also grow increasingly diverse. So the question is Can we burn this fuel? Can we get maximum corporate power from the diverse work we're now drawing into the system?' We as an organisation are trying to create an environment where we can burn 'that fuel', where people feel that they are valued and belong.

If you substitute the word 'society' for 'corporation', it raises a question for all of us. We are, I believe, in a time of unprecedented change in Irish society. Our population is becoming more diverse, people have higher expectations of work, and indeed of life. Their lifestyles are changing. We need to create a more inclusive Ireland that is accepting of difference, in both our communites and our workplaces.

This does not happen overnight. I would like to ask each of you leaving here today to take some time to think about this and to consider what you, personally, can do to make Ireland more inclusive. Everyone can make a difference!

BUSINESS AS A MEANS, NOT AN END

John Liddy

Can I just say at the outset that Roche does not have a grand plan nor are they experts in the subject of human relations. The purpose of my speech is to share with you some initiatives that are taking place within Roche.

I suppose it is fair to say that private business has seldom been as celebrated or lauded as it is today. Market liberalisation, deregulation and privatisation take up a significant part of our daily news. However, in spite of that, while business reigns supreme, questions are being asked as to what business is for. These questions are being asked by Mr and Mrs Citizen, who, in addition to being workers, may also be shareholders.

The purpose of economic and social life cannot be solely to play host to successful business. The maximisation of shareholder value, or the single-minded pursuit of economic efficiency, cannot become ends in themselves. Other human values – the need to sustain families, to treat men and women equally, to look after the environment, to respect natural justice, to allow dignity in the workplace – also require expression and are the end to which successful business is the means. In other words, business is a means, not an end.

The environment in which business operates has changed dramatically. Employees are more assertive about their rights at work. Their expectations have changed. We have seen a dramatic increase in the number of aid agencies and pressure groups. A recent UK report showed an increase in the number of NGO's (Non Government Organisations) from 1,400 in 1970 to 28,900 in the '90s. Being a multinational healthcare company, Roche is not immune or exempt from these influences.

I would like now to share with you some initiatives that we have put in place at Roche. At a corporate level, like many companies, we have established a set of guiding principles, which embody our vision

and the kind company that we strive to be. These define our
relationships with various stakeholders (employees, community,
environment, customers). I am sure all of you are familiar with
mission statements, customer charters, etc., which you will see in
many company reception areas. Obviously it is much more
challenging to translate these mission/value statements into action. In
Roche, in order to ensure that we live up to our guiding principles, we
have incorporated these as part of our performance management
system. In the past, we had set goals for management and staff and
measured performance only against the achievement of these goals. We
now also include a review of these goals against Roche's guiding
principles. In other words, we measure performance not only in terms
of what people have done, but how they have achieved these results.

We have introduced a worldwide training programme for all
managers called 'Behaviour at Roche'. This programme is very much
focused on business ethics. It involves the use of case studies
representing typical ethical dilemmas that may arise in our business. A
key part of this programme is central monitoring to ensure that all
managers participate. Again, the major focus of this initiative is to
bring values and principles into practice as opposed to just having
written policies.

I would like now to talk briefly about some community and
employee initiatives that have taken place in our plant in Clarecastle.
Recognising the need to have open communication with community in
recent years, we have set up a Community Liaison Group with local
residents. The key aspect of this group is its independence. It is chaired
by a member of the community and consists of some company
representatives and key members of the local community. All topics
that have a potential to impact the community are discussed at
meetings that are held three or four times per year. We have a policy of
encouraging our employees to get involved with community initiatives
and we provide support to them where possible. The following is an
example of two of these projects.

The first is an American sourced programme called Junior
Achievement. Each year, approximately six volunteers work with local
schools with special focus on interpersonal skills and an appreciation
of the role of business. They deal with aptitude and possible career

choices. A subtext of this programme is to influence kids who may be contemplating leaving the system. It has also been a source of development for our staff – teaching a subject to a group of children and perhaps gaining a better understanding of the challenges teachers are facing.

The second initiative, called School Links, also involves school visits, with emphasis on career opportunities. It also involves having a number of teachers spend some time in the company with the purpose of understanding the various roles within the company. We also facilitate school visits and open days to try to create a better understanding of our systems and processes.

Technology without people is not very effective, as Fr Harry mentioned last night. I will now talk a little about our Employee Development Programme. As a company we very much support continuous learning. In the past, our focus was on task-related training. In more recent years we have broadened this to include personal development and have also put a large emphasis on accreditation. We have seen some initial results from this approach. Employees are more open to and in some cases seek change. We are seeing a higher degree of confidence as they believe their skills are more portable and less dependent on the company.

Recently, all of our senior management group participated in a Covey Leadership programme. As you know from Covey's presentation last year, Covey focuses very much on balance between work and other roles in society. Our plan is to develop internal facilitators to take this through all levels of the organisation. We believe this is a worthwhile investment and will benefit the company. It is our wish that this will make all of us more effective in our other roles in society – as parents, neighbours, etc. We would like to believe that these skills have led to higher job satisfaction.

As with all major organisations, communication at Roche is a significant challenge. A number of initiatives have helped in this area. We have committed to communicating good and bad news in a timely manner and not leaving it to the grapevine. For this we use a formal team-briefing method, which involves communicating the same message to all employees within a defined period. Completion of this briefing is monitored continually with feedback sought from all briefers. The result of this has been to increase the overall trust level and has, to a large extent, eliminated the view of management manipulation of information, for example, all bad news during union negotiations.

Finally, I would like to talk about consultation. We are seeing what is a very positive development, a greater demand for consultation, more of an approach of competing responsibilities as opposed to competing rights as referred to by Maureen yesterday. We have joint working groups working two key topics: a) Training, which is focused on key skills required for the future, and b) Team working, which has the objective of increased empowerment of individual groups.

We have also recently commenced a strategic review of our business, involving typical SWOT (strength, weakness, opportunities, threats) analysis. Again, with objective of maximum consultation and ownership, we have involved all our employees in this process. We believe the output from these groups will be much more acceptable and easier to implement because of the involvement of people affected.

I hope I have given you a small sense of what is happening at Roche. As I indicated in my introduction, business and its relationship with community, employees and customers is changing dramatically. This will require a change in paradigm for all of us. This paradigm shift behoves us to see ourselves as an integral part of the community in which we live and to see ourselves as a major influence in the lives and well-being of our employees.

With greater power and freedom comes greater responsibility and accountability. I believe we are just at the very early stages of this rapid change but we ignore it at our peril.

Putting People at the Centre of Things

Robert E. Lane

A Parable

On the way to the conference with my wife, Helen, an economist stopped me in a casual, friendly fashion and asked me how much I would take for my wife.

'She is not for sale,' I said.

He was disappointed, of course, but persisted: 'I understand,' he said, 'but have you had her appraised recently – you know, the way art objects are appraised?'

'She is priceless,' I said, 'whatever Christie's or Sotheby's might assess her for.'

'Do you not have her insured?' asked the economist.

'Yes, she has some life insurance,' I said, 'but that figure does not represent her value to me.'

The economist was sceptical and tried another approach. 'Think of the opportunity costs,' he said. 'With the laws being what they are, being married to Helen means that you cannot also be married to, say, Betty Grable, Hedy Lamar, or Judy Garland.' (It seems he was about my age.)

'I think of my marriage as settled and hence without opportunity costs.' I said. 'My utility preference schedule just happens to work that way and I minimise regret.'

Kant put it differently. People, he said, have *dignity.* Everything else can be exchanged and hence has only *value.* People cannot be exchanged.

On the Threshold of a New Humanism?

We are on the threshold of a promising historical period when the values that have brought us to new peaks of affluence are no longer serviceable, a period fundamentally different from the industrial age that extended our lives and educated so many of us. This new era has been called 'the post-industrial society,' because of the shift in jobs

131

from the industrial to the service section, and a 'postmodern society,' because of the shift from material, scarcity values to quality of life values. These terms address the point of departure, where we are leaving from; I will call it the 'New Humanism' because it promises to put humans and humanistic values at the center of things. Advanced economies, like Ireland riding on the back of the Celtic Tiger, are now on the threshold of this New Humanism. We are all caught up in a monumental struggle to cross that threshold, at the confluence of powerful forces urging us on and equally powerful forces holding us back. The outcome is uncertain so let us see what forces are at work.

Valuing Human Beings

Let me suggest three ways of evaluating human beings: Aristotelian, religious-humanistic, and economic. The Aristotelian way, which also follows one of the modern philosophical formulae for assigning value, relies on concepts of the essence of good human character. Just as a knife is a good knife if it does well the things that knives are supposed to do, so in Aristotelian terms, a person is a good person if he (or she) performs well the functions of personhood (or, for Aristotle, of good citizenship). A person does this by possessing the virtues characteristic of better people, that is, if in the sphere of 'fear and confidence' a person shows neither rashness nor cowardice, but rather courage; or if in the sphere of 'getting and spending' the person shows neither vulgarity nor pettiness, but magnificence, that person is to be valued more highly.[1]

But this way of evaluating human beings is culture-bound and gives them no intrinsic value; their value is contingent on the grades they earn from some philosopher judge.

The second way of valuing people has two modes, the religious and the humanistic. In the West, the Christian religious mode is the older and is more persuasive to more people. It says that human beings are endowed with souls that, because they are divinely given, are of infinite, rather than contingent, value. The second mode is the humanistic one, expressed by Kant: because people cannot be exchanged for each other, they have unique value or 'dignity'.[2] Although uniqueness is a weak source of ultimate value, like the religious argument for human value it is not contingent on the performances of people.

That the Christian religion carries the blemish of having supported slavery and torture of heretics is insufficinet reason to say that it does not *now* offer support for the intrinsic value of *all* human beings, but it has the disadvantages of failing to appeal to Muslims, Buddhists, Hindus and pagans. In this sense, humanism is more universal. But both the relgious and the humanistic sources of evaluation of human beings endow humankind with intrinsic value. In that sense they contrast with both the Aristotelian and the economistic mode of evaluation. Whatever their deficencies, they are essential to counter the prevailing economic evaluation of human beings.

In an economistic society, to put human beings at the centre of things they must have economic value. In economic terms, humans have two kinds of value: as *producer goods* their value may be measured by their lifetime economic product, which, in a perfect market, is the same as their lifetime earnings. As *consumer goods* they must yield utility or satisfaction to someone directly, the level of satisfaction being measured by what someone is willing to pay for their company, or perhaps just for their being. That someone, of course, could be the self – how much would one pay for one's own ransom?

There is good news on the producer goods front. People are worth more today than ever before. In his studies of investing in people, the Nobel laureate economist, Theodore Schultz, says: 'The thrust of my argument is that investment in population quality and in knowledge in large part determines the future prospects of mankind.'[3] This outcome, he says, is because the returns to human capital are now larger than the returns to physical capital in both advanced and developing countries. However one calculates the economic value of people, according to their contribution to economic productivity, according to their earning power, or according to the investment in their training, people are economically more valuable today. Here, indeed, is progress: each prime minister is more valuable than his predecessor!

(1) People are more valuable by measures of their replacement value, the life insurance they hold. In current dollars in 1980 in the United States, the per household dollar value of life insurance was $41,900; thirteen years later in 1993, that per household value was $111,600. Allowing for inflation, the value of people had about

doubled over the period. By this measure, however, in the eighteenth century before there was such a thing as life insurance, people were valueless. When people die these days, they are worth more than they were in the past. Indeed, some people, particularly those who yield negative value to their friends, are worth more dead than alive – in the funeral director's refrigerator they are frozen assets.

(2) People are more durable these days, but for about forty years they have not extended their working lives to keep pace with their increased durability, and hence the period in which their human capital has a positive yield is no longer than it was when they were less durable, unlike their worth in the funeral director's refrigerator, their value may not be increased by their durability. In one sense, longevity reduces the value of human beings because the period of their lives when they consume more than they produce is extended. All that human capital is wasted.

(3) People's consumer value, the direct yield to self and others, is something else. By these consumer utility standards, the value of people has probably not increased over the generations. At any one time, however, the more friends a person has (and the fewer enemies), the more valuable he or she is. It is very hard to assess this value because there is no market mechanism to help, but like some economists, one could imagine an auction whereby people could bid for a person's friendship and, if he happened to have rich friends, he might turn out to be a very valuable person even if not a rich or productive person himself. Cultivating rich friends for this imaginary auction in retirement, or perhaps much earlier, would certainly be the rational course for the person concerned about his or her value.

(4) Are children worth more or less in postmodern society? The productive value of an infant is the projected life-time earnings less the cost of rearing and educating that growing infant to maturity. (Swift's 'modest proposal' enhanced the value of infants who otherwise had only negative value.) The consumer value of a child is the utilities he or she directly provides to parents, siblings, schoolmates and itself. When children were explicitly production goods, their value was clear. Thus, Adam Smith speaks admiringly of the economic value of children in North America, where, he said, 'the labour of each child, before it can leave [the parents' house], is computed to be worth a

hundred pounds clear gain to them,' with the added virtue that this promotes marriage for widows, for 'the value of children is the greatest of all encouragements to marriage'.[4] But in postmodern society, children are primarily expensive consumer goods who must yield much higher direct utilities to their parents to justify their existence.

Today there is mixed evidence on the value of children to their parents. On the one hand it is clear that couples are generally happier before the children are born and after they leave the nest,[5] but, on the other hand, of the things that people report they like doing best, playing with their own children ranks very high, much higher than watching television or sports.[6] A clever economist might take care of these mixed findings by providing a 'rent-a-child' programme, but I do not think it would work: the same study that found that playing with one's own children was a delight found that taking care of other people's children ranked at the very bottom of the list of things people enjoyed doing.

On the whole, I find that, sadly, the value of chilren has declined in postmodern society, partly because they are no longer producers of goods, partly because the same welfare state that raised the value of older persons makes unnecessary the support of these pensioners by their children, and partly, perhaps, because a materialist society makes childcare less 'profitable' than does market work by mothers. Hence, says the economist, fewer children are produced in advanced societies, which are no longer reproducing themselves.

One further note on the value of children. One might have thought that when the supply declines, the value would rise, but since children have negative economic value during their immaturity, and since the demand for items with negative current value depends on expected future value, the value of children is greatly influenced by the stage of the business cycle and by expectations of economic growth. Along with everything else, economic growth increases the value of children.

(5) Women are more valuable now than when they did not do so much market work. Of course, this changed valuation is an artefact of the way GNP has been calculated (when a man marries his housekeeper she may do the same work as before but because she ceases being paid her contribution to GNP is zero). If a mother

neglects her small child in order to work as a secretary, she becomes more valuable than if she stayed home to care for her toddler. In this kind of case, it may be said that the toddlers of this world pay for the rise in GNP in all countries. But from another perspective, the same Ted Schultz who found the value of human populations to be increasing argues that the education of women is the best investment in developing countries because educated women are better mothers; they talk to their children and monitor their healthcare better than uneducated, village-bound mothers. Women are more valuable both because they represent greater investments, which gives them value both at home and in the market, and because the demand for their services has increased.

From these many perspectives it seems that people are more valuable in postindustrial society than in traditional or industrial societies. The analysis is only partly facetious, for in any move from an economistic or materialist society to a humanistic society the point of departure is important. If people are economically more valuable, they will receive more education, and more education leads to less materialistic values.[7] But from my point of view, measuring the value of people by their earning capacities or how much is invested in them is exactly the wrong way to proceed. It violates the philosophical as well as the religious injunction to treat people as ends, to assign to them intrinsic value. And because self-esteem is largely independent of level of income,[8] money values tell us little about how people value themselves – although, perniciously, level of income is a default value in assessing the character of others.[9] If the transition to a more humanistic society is made easier by the higher value of individuals in a materialist society, it is made more difficult by the lingering material evaluation of persons.

I turn now to another kind of argument: what happens to the value of *money* when money is relatively more plentiful and other goods, like companionship, are relatively less plentiful?

Money vs. People: The Declining Marginal Utility of Money

In this millennium year, on average, the material standard of living of people in Northern Europe and North America is about four times greater than that of their grandparents and at least eight times greater than that of their forebears at the start of the industrial revolution. Under these unprecedented circumstances, it is not surprising that people's values and preferences have changed. Indeed, economic theory holds that when one good becomes relatively more abundant than others, that good will yield diminishing rates of satisfaction; in the language of economists, it will offer diminishing marginal utility (DMU). What economists did not anticipate is that the alternative goods that become more appealing are not things you can buy in the market, rather, they are things like friendship and family felicity. As money and what you can buy with money become relatively more abundant compared to these non-market goods, the relative value of money declines and the relative value of people and their companionship increases. This is a crucial point to which I will return later.

Why companionship? It is an alternative approach to the value of people, why they, rather than money, should be put at the centre of things. Applying the above DMU principle, extending it to the money versus companionship trade-off, and borrowing Jefferson's language, I hold these propositions to be self-evident:

(1) that people have multiple sources of happiness and satisfaction and will seek a variety of goods in their pursuits of happiness;

(2) that (above the poverty level) the goods that contribute most to happiness, such as companionship and intrinsic work enjoyment, are not priced, do not pass through the market, and (less obviously) have inadequate shadow prices;

(3) that as any one good becomes relatively more abundant the satisfactions people get from that good usually (but not universally) wanes in relation to the satisfactions they get from other goods.

(4) that, therefore, when people and societies become richer, they will receive declining satisfaction from each new unit of income and increasing satisfaction from such other goods as companionship and intrinsic work satisfaction;

(5) that, as a corollary to propositions 3 and 4, when companionship is abundant, the power of new companions to yield satisfaction will also diminish compared to the power of money;[10]

(6) that, as historical and social circumstances change, the power of the various available goods (e.g., income, companionship, work

satisfaction) to yield satisfaction will change with the changes in the supply of each good (as well as with changing taste).

One of the implications of these propositions is that the specialists of any agency, such as the market or democracy or family, inevitably deal with a limited range of the goods thought to yield satisfaction during any given historical period and, therefore, by themselves are inadequate guides to maximising subjective well-being (SWB). Since (above the poverty level) the goods that contribute most to happiness and life-satisfaction do not pass through the market and are not priced, specialists in markets are useful but marginal advisers on how to achieve a high quality of life. (That economists should be custodians of that kind of satisfaction called 'utility' is a grotesque accident of the history of science.) Other specialists are similarly useful but also similarly marginal: democratic theorists, advocates of this or that religion, specialists in family life, social workers, and so forth.

Now I want very briefly to reveal how these considerations influence our assessment of income and companionship in contributing to subjective well-being. Essentially, the discussion documents the theory of diminishing returns mentioned earlier and in propositions 2 and 3.

Income

Proposition 3 says that when money is scarce, it yields a generous bounty of SWB, but as money becomes more plentiful, that yield declines. Cross-cultural studies including many Third World countries show, as everyone would expect, that as countries get richer, the average level of SWB increases. But, as Ruut Veenhoven reports,[11] within this large, heterogeneous group of countries, there are diminishing hedonic returns to income as per capita income rises. Among the relatively rich countries of Europe, this attenuation of the power of money to buy happiness is even more clear[12] and in the United States there is some evidence of an actual decline of joy as the economy prospered in the post-war years.[13] I take this composite picture to mean that the relationship between income and happiness in developing countries is substantial but in advanced countries it is probably about zero. This is a case of diminishing hedonic returns to increasing income.

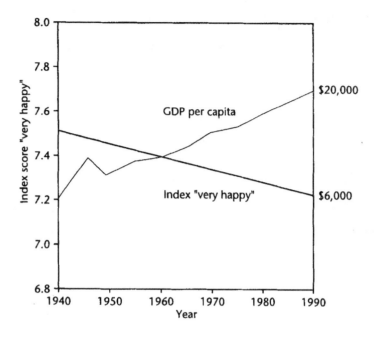

Sources: Percent 'very happy' various surveys, courtesy of Ed Diener, GDP per capita in constant 1987 dollars: U.S. Bureau of Economic Analysis; *Statistical Abstract of the United States, 1995.* Washington, DC; Bureau of the Census, 1995

Figure 1: Index of 'Very Happy' and GDP per capita 1946–1990

Companionship

My thesis holds that in any trade-off between the two goods, money and companionship, where money is relatively plentiful and companionship relatively scarce, companionship will add more to SWB than money. In reverse, where money is relatively scarce and companionship relatively plentiful, money will add more to SWB. If I can show that this is the case, the thesis is by no means verified, but it is not falsified. Let us see.

Two American quality of life studies[14] show that satisfying family life plus relations with friends contribute more to measures of SWB than do satisfaction with standard of living.[15] Companionship (especially family life) makes a larger contribution to happiness than does income. To the extent that the declining marginal utility of money is based on opportunity costs (the cost of what is given up by money-making activities), one might infer that it is the lost opportunities for companionship that is doing much of the work of undermining the power of money to make people happy.

First, to test whether or not companionship is increasingly scarce, I have taken the General Social Survey (GSS) record of visiting relations with parents, kin, neighbors and friends over the 1972–1994 period. In fact, visiting with parents, siblings, relatives, and neighbours have all declined,[16] a partial confirmation of the Maine-Tönnies-Weber theses regarding the change in human relations in the modern period. In the West, these companionships are in relatively and increasingly short supply. As indicated by surveys of satisfaction, demand has not declined.

And second, to test whether companionship has lower hedonic returns when it is abundant, compare the relation between companionship and SWB in Western individualist countries, where companionship is scarce, with mostly Asian collectivist or interdependent societies where it is abundant. As it turned out, 'the size of the relations between friendship satisfaction and life satisfaction was strongly dependent on the degree of individualism of the country, with the correlation between friendship satisfaction stronger in individualistic countries.'[17] That is, where companionship is abundant, it makes less of a contribution to SWB than where it is scarce, as in the United States. Also, as predicted, among the poorer collectivist countries, money makes more of a contribution to SWB than among the richer collectivist countries.[18] Beyond that, a supplementary theory of optimal balance between companionship and income is indicated. For a time, the economically successful Asian countries of the Pacific rim seemed to serve as possible models, but the post 1997 record seems to show that where market imperatives and familistic preferences collide, the market will win.[19]

Materialism on the Humanist Threshold

The declining marginal utility of income is reason enough to reduce our economism, but there is another reason why material goods do not satisfy people – and perhaps never did: people who make money a central feature of their lives are not happy.

Individual Materialism

Can a market economy maximize well-being? Perhaps there is something intrinsic to market economies that limits the ability of their participants to achieve that state of grace. The irony will not be missed: markets have been defended largely because of their capacity to maximize utility or well-being, that is, to permit one to pursue happiness in one's own way and thus, within one's budgetary constraints, find that road that leads to one's individualised well-being. Intrinsic limits in the system would spoil that idyll.

The orientation that concerns us is the kind of materialism where money and the goods it buys are the central values that inform career choices and personal striving. Along these lines, Marsha Richins and her associates have developed measures of materialism, which they characterized as follows: 'We considered materialism to be a set of centrally held beliefs about the importance of possessions in one's life and measured the three belief-domains: acquisition centrality, the role of acquisition in happiness, and the role of possessions in defining success.'[20] One grasps these principles better when the actual questions that measure these values and beliefs are given. Here is a sample from Richins and Dawson's 18 item measure:

Success
'I admire people who own expensive homes, cars, and clothes.'
'Some of the most important achievements in life include acquiring material possessions.'

Centrality
'I usually buy only the things I need.' (reverse scoring)
'I enjoy spending money on things that aren't practical.'
'Buying things gives me a lot of pleasure.'

Happiness
'I have all the things I really need to enjoy life.' (reverse scoring)
'My life would be better if I owned certain things I don't have.'
'I wouldn't be any happier if I owned nicer things.' (reverse scoring)
'I'd be happier if I could afford to buy more things.'
'It sometimes bothers me quite a bit that I can't afford to buy all the things I'd like.'

Source: Marsha Richins and Scott Dawson. 1992. 'A Consumer Values Orientation for Materialism and its Measurement: Scale Development and Validation.' *Journal of Consumer Research* 19: 303–316 at 310. I have oversampled the happiness questions because of our interest in the effects of materialism on well-being.

Table 1. Richins and Dawson's Items Measuring Materialism

It is time to examine what economists have always assumed, namely that greed (or material self-interest) is both the motive that makes the market work (which is partly true) and the motive that leads to maximum individual well-being (which is often false). In their study of materialism, Richins and Dawson included questions on people's satisfaction with: their lives, the amount of fun they were having, family life, friends, and their standards of living. As it turned out, 'materialism was negatively related to satisfaction in all aspects of life measured,' with the strongest relationship with satisfaction with standards of living (-.39), closely followed by the fun people were having (-.34) and with their friendship satisfaction (-.31). The weakest relation was with their satisfaction with their family life (-.17),[21] always the most autonomous area of any of the domains of life. Taking up a causal ordering question, the authors present evidence that materialism is not the effect of unhappiness, but rather is more likely its cause.

Tim Kasser and Richard Ryan's several studies are totally supportive. Using tested measures of psychological adjustment, 'vitality,' depression, and anxiety, they found that: 'Placing money high in the rank ordering [of goals] was associated with less vitality, more depression ($r2 = .28$, $p < .01$) and more anxiety ($r2 = .22$, $p < .05$). In contrast, 'the relative centrality of self-acceptance and affiliation [value of good relations with others] was related to less anxiety and depression.'[22]

A study of college alumni (not students) will help to confirm this relationship between materialism and unhappiness. 'Among 800 alumni of Hobart and William Smith Colleges, those who preferred a high income and occupational success and prestige to having very close friends and a close marriage were twice as likely as their fellow alumni to describe themselves as 'fairly' or 'very' unhappy.'[23]

Following economic theory, from time to time I have referred to material *self-interest* but have not introduced any evidence that materialists are more self-interested than others. In fact, they are. Asked how they would spend a windfall of $20,000, materialists would spend three times as much as non-materialists on themselves, would contribute less to charity or their churches, and give less than half as much to friends and family.[24] Materialist *self*-interest is a fair description.

Why Are Materialists Unhappy?

Why is materialism in a materialist, consumer-driven society, associated not with well-being but with ill-being? Materialism is a set of values and, perhaps, a set of personality traits; it is not a description limited to those in materialistic occupations – businessmen, merchants, salespeople, and so forth. Many of the studies of materialism deal with students with no other settled occupation; also many of the qualities described can be found in the professions, the arts, and among intellectuals. But one thing seems clear: materialist unhappiness does not stem from poverty. In the Richins and Dawson study, the correlation of materialism with income was .04 (NS) and in the Kasser and Ryan studies it was almost zero.[25] Why the dissatisfaction and unhappiness? Scholars have offered a number of explanations:

(1) Happiness is associated with pursuit of intrinsic, not extrinsic goals like fame and money, goals characterised by less reliance on the approval of others and by more self-acceptance, good relations with others, desire to help the community, and physical fitness and good health.[26]

(2) Because their activities rely on extrinsic rewards materialists are inevitably dependent on rewards controlled by others.[27] Thus, they lack the benefits of self-rewards and self-direction that come from reliance on intrinsic, non-contingent pleasures.[28]

(3) People who work for money may enjoy outcome satisfactions without process satisfactions, pleasure in doing the job itself. For example, people who work primarily for pay are somehow marked by low self-esteem and anxiety and have lower job satisfaction than those with mixed motives.[29]

(4) Unlike other goods, such as glory (athletes and warriors), piety (monks and priests), a satisfied conscience, or companionship, money and commodities have limited powers to yield pleasure. As Durkheim, Lange, and Pufendorf all believed, the appetite for material goods is more *insatiable* than the desire for these other kinds of goods.[30] The reason for this distinction between the power of money and of other goods to yield pleasure is not self-explanatory. The cause of the difference, I believe, is not so much insatiability *per se*, as that, unlike other goods, money is both an input (earned) and an output (spent).

Consequently, it is possible to want to spend more than one earns – a sure prescription for misery, as Micawber once explained to David Copperfield. Thus, Sirgy suggests that 'this proclivity to overconsume and underproduce may be partly responsible for materialists' inflated and value-laden expectations of their standard of living.'[31] Furthermore, money is thought to offer a passport to all other pleasures, which it does not – as in piety, a good conscience, and gratifying companionship.

(5) Many Americans are *ambivalent* about their values and goals.[32] For example, it was possible in 1973 for American students simultaneously to 'welcome less emphasis on money (80%) and to list 'the money you earn' among their most 'important objectives (61%)'[33] Thus, it is the priority given to material things more than their absolute lack of value that makes materialists' lives unrewarding.[34]

(6) If the values and practices of materialists provides us with a clue to their relative unhappiness, the character of materialists may offer further clues. For example, Belk and his associates have found a syndrome of envy, nongenerosity, and possessiveness that are associated with unhappiness.[35]

(7) Other evidence suggests that a person who places special value on material things ranks lower on a measure of ego development.[36]

(8) Materialists are *socially awkward*, that is, 'materialists have poorer social adjustment and mental health' than others.[37] The unhappiness of materialists, therefore, is not explained only by their unrewarding values but also by their low social skills and psychological distress. Also, (9) their recreational activities are more passive than others'. Materialists watch a lot more TV, an activity that most studies show is not really enjoyed very much (e.g., less than gardening or cooking).[38] In contrast, non-materialists are more likely to spend time socialising with others or planning for their own futures, activities that are usually (but not always) more enjoyable.[39]

What Hope For A New Humanism?

Which societies are likely to be the most and the least materialist as defined above by Richins and Dawson?

Trends in Materialism

Following Polanyi,[40] I suggest that primitive societies are least materialistic; then the post-industrial societies in which we are living,[41] then peasant or traditional societies (Tönnies' *gemeinschaft!*), and most materialistic would be industrialising societies whose members have just discovered that they can influence degrees of wealth (as Montesquieu said). The idea that in the post-industrialist societies materialism declines reminds us of Keynes' belief that, when we are rich enough: 'The love of money as a possession – as distinguished from the love of money as a means to the enjoyments and realities of life – will be recognised for what it is, a somewhat disgusting morbidity, one of those semi-criminal, semi-pathological propensities which one hands over with a shudder to the specialists in mental disease.'[42]

Was Keynes Right?

Hyperbole? Certainly; the old fox was teasing his colleagues. But perhaps he was also dimly perceiving the hedonic irrationality that social scientists now have documented. Even though people are slow to learn their own best interests, as we enter deeper into the Threshold, 'rational' people will seek other goods and materialism will decline, will it not? The evidence is discouraging. If we look at changes in student values, we find no such rational process. A remarkably long series on personal goals and values of freshmen in American colleges pairs two values, materialist desire to seek wealth as a career versus a desire 'to develop a meaningful life philosophy'. Note, first, the gradual decline of materialism and the rise of a 'meaningful philosophy' for a decade to about 1978, then the reversal of these trends for a ten year period until about 1987, followed by a high plateau for the next seven years to 1994.[43] Among American college freshmen over this period materialism has certainly not declined.

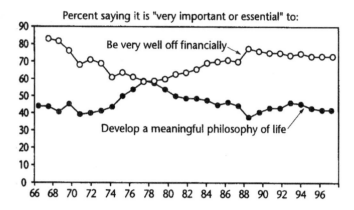

Source: Annual surveys of 200,000+ entering American colleges annually as published in *The American Freshman* (Los Angeles: Higher Education Research Institute, UCLA). Figure created by David Myers and reproduced with his kind permission).

Figure 2: Goal Materialism among US College Freshmen: Percent saying it is 'very important or essential' to 'Be very well off financially or saying to 'Develop a meaningful philosophy of life', 1966–96.

Inglehart offers a second measure of materialism, one that deals with policy priorities: in capsule form, compared to postmaterialists, materialists are more likely to favour maintaining a stable economy, economic growth, maintaining order, and fighting against crime. In contrast, compared to materialists, postmaterialists favour a less impersonal society, more 'say' on the job, more say in government, and a society where ideas count more than money.[44] There are mixed categories whose responses include support for items from both groups. The postmaterialist values certainly reflect the values that we would expect to find in the New Humanist order. Postmaterialism, says Inglehart, increases when a new generation brought up in peace and relative economic security reaches maturity.

Although postmaterialism increased more rapidly than materialism in the US from 1972 to 1992, a closer look shows that Inglehart's policy materialism rose rapidly in the 1970s and, with the exception of 1984, maintained a fairly high plateau in the 1988–1992 period. Both time series for student materialist goals and adult policy materialism show a period of rising materialism to the late 1980s followed by a period of high, stable materialism into the 1990s. Are there limits to the development of a New Humanist order in a market society? Is there a *ceiling effect?*

Does Rising Humanism Encounter a Ceiling?

Looking at the pattern of change of postmaterialism in Europe, Elinor Scarborough suggests that when materialists (and their mixed categories in the four-question scale) fall to about 75–80% (still, obviously, the overwhelming majority of the population), their decline is somehow arrested. This pattern of change, says Scarborough, 'suggests that some ceiling effect is at work: below the 20% level, postmaterialism continues to progress; above a level of 20–25%, further advances seem fragile.'[45]

The pattern is just the opposite of the one I am suggesting: at a high level of affluence and education (and the materialism that produced it) the opportunity costs of materialism become too high and then, and only then, do the alternatives to materialism seem widely attractive. But the time series suggests that this is true only up to a point when something blocks that defection from materialism. What might that be?

One suggestion is the increase of women (who tend to be less materialistic than men)[46] and adolescents in the labour force where contingent reinforcement and the value of money in what they do increases their materialism. That is, as countries become richer they once again enlist women and youth in the work force. Or perhaps the occupations in which non-materialists are happiest (teaching? social work? civil service? research and development? the performing arts – outside of Hollywood – ?) are in limited supply.[47] Perhaps it is not possible to find round holes for the round pegged non-materialists, but the alternatives are not promising: Shopkeepers and small businesspeople are less happy than people in other similarly rewarded occupations[48] and managers are more anxious about their futures than are professionals.[49]

I suspect that market economies simply require that most of the population enter careers that demand for their gratification some love of money; that is how they are designed and regulated. However, as Frank Knight observed, many participants 'do not like the [market] game at all and rebel against being compelled to play it and against being estimated socially and personally on the basis of their success or failure.'[50] So the materialist is a 'realist' and adopts the values that he thinks must be adopted to 'play the game' – and doesn't, in the end, find satisfaction. 'Realism' of this kind takes the form of searching for happiness where it is least likely to be found.

What hope, then, for a society where people, or humanist values more generally, are more important than money? We turn again to the innovative economist John Maynard Keynes who anticipated the time when technology and the magical powers of compound interest would make us rich enough to shed the materialist motives of market economies. In fact, we are economically already where Keynes expected us to be in a hundred years, but, perhaps because of market pressures and the slow progress of cultural change, we have not adapted as Keynes thought we should. We are still only on the threshold of the New Humanism he projected and still only timidly experimenting with 'the arts of life' that Keynes advised seventy years ago.[51]

We have encountered a disturbing dilemma: materialism does not make people happy but the market whose fruitfulness makes it possible to value non-material goods imposes limits on the kinds of careers and values that would be more satisfying. 'In the sweat of thy brow shalt thou eat bread.' (Gen 14:19.) Shall we never cross the Threshold of the New Humanism?

False Starts and New Beginnings

Matter vs. mind; things vs. people; economic growth vs. human growth: the dichotomies have meaning only after the basic necessities of life are assured. And now they are assured – but before celebrating, recall Friedrich Engels on the same topic 110 years ago:

> The struggle for individual existence comes to an end and at this point, in a certain sense, man finally cuts himself off from the animal world, leaves the conditions of animal existence behind him and enters conditions which are really human, . . . becomes for the first time the real conscious master of nature. . . . It is humanity's leap from the realm of necessity into the realm of freedom.

And that realm of freedom is, in fact, a form of the New Humanism for it 'guarantees to everyone the completely unrestricted development and exercise of their physical and mental faculties – this possibility now exists for the first time, but it does exist.'[52] The result was the Soviet dystopia.

Thus cautioned, we seek an emergent model, a vision of the near future that clings to more or less successful institutions of the past and builds upon their successes. How to put people at the centre of things without destroying the material world that has brought them to this point?

Postmodernity as the New Humanism

Something is happening outside the United States, often a humanisticly backward country, that promises relief. In Inglehart's World Value Survey data, there is evidence of the development of a postmodernity stage that is markedly different from the modernity that we know so well. It is marked not only by the postmaterialist values mentioned above, but includes diminished priority for economic efficiency and growth, rejection of both religious authority and absolute moral values (circumstances make a difference), tolerance for ethnic minorities and for deviance from sexual and other norms, and an emphasis on better human relations and warm communal ties. Beyond these qualities, postmodernity shares with modernity an emphasis on individual autonomy and reliance on the informative value of a person's own experience as contrasted to orthodoxies of all kinds.[53] What of the ceiling effect? Inglehart finds that the richer the country and the younger the cohort, the more the emphasis on postmodern values. The Scandinavian countries and the Netherlands have achieved higher postmaterialist value rankings than the US[54] where materialist values linger at a high level. The conversion from materialism to postmaterialism and from modernity to postmodernity does slow down as nations become more wealthy, but apparently that movement does not stop at the level achieved in the United States at the turn of the century.

If the market is itself a stumbling block on the threshold of the New Humanism, is nature another such obstacle? In violating economic laws do we also violate natural laws?

Nature's Priorities

We are a long way from the time when the chief agent of 'progress' was natural selection, but we carry in our genes the instructions that guided us in that journey. Do these instructions help or hinder the movement to the New Humanism?

Fighting and Mating

There are two meanings to Spencer's term, 'the survival of the fittest': the one that survived Darwin for a hundred years is the selection of those whose foraging and fighting skills gave sufficient advantage to their physical survival to enable them to outbreed rivals. The more recent modification of this interpretation, made famous by Dawkins' *The Selfish Gene*, focuses on qualities that are sufficiently more attractive to the other sex as to give a breeding advantage to any variant of the species who has these qualities, even if the variant individuals are somewhat inept at food gathering – hence the peacock. In capsule form, the first emphasises fighting and the second 'making love,' perhaps (species differ) after fighting for the right to make love. 'Making love' (copulation) releases the hormones vasopressin in males and oxytocin in females, which have the general effect of making all conspecifics seem more congenial, lovable and encourage parenting behaviour.[55] Also, through kin selection, altruism involving self-sacrifice may be advantageous for the group in the processes of natural selection. Finally, dominance, especially in female hierarchies, often seems to retard gene proliferation.[56] It is not the case that our genes carry only those instructions appropriate for 'nature red in tooth and claw.'

If our inherited foraging motives and skills in market or other societies are not always the most important, what are? There are certain clues that suggest that the first and primary drive among primates, and perhaps all mammals (and social insects?) are conspecific relationships.

> Infants are born with or acquire early a number of abilities and dispositions that will help them learn about people. They find human faces, voices, and movements particularly interesting stimuli to attend and respond to. They also possess and further

develop impressive abilities to perceptually analyze and discriminate human stimuli. . . . There is also evidence that infants respond differently to people than they do to objects and seem to expect people to behave differently than objects do.[57]

For example, they imitate people but not movements of objects. Furthermore, those people who process faces and objects in the same areas of the brain turn out to be autistic.[58] At least one kind of materialism is organically different from this perceptual humanism. (As a side issue, we may observe that if responsiveness to people, as contrasted to things, is 'normal,' then women are more normal than men.)[59] Something about people gives whatever is human a salience and preference in the perceptual system. On the basis of the findings of eleven studies, David Sears reports 'that attitude objects are evaluated more favourably the more they resemble individual human beings. Because perceived similarity . . . increase[s] liking, individual persons . . . attract more favorable evaluations than . . . less personal attitude objects, such as inanimate objects or even aggregated or grouped versions of the same persons.'[60] Psychology has rediscovered the emotions. In a cross-cultural exploration of the emotions of joy, sadness, anger, and fear, Klaus Scherer reports that all the major emotions are stimulated primarily by social relationships. 'It is rather well established by now that such relationship needs are central components of the motivational make-up of most social animals.'[61] Finally, people will endure a higher level of pain for the approval of others than they will for money.[62] And with social support, people are more healthy, less likely to succumb to stress, and live longer.

Because human stimuli heighten perception, elicit approval, arouse emotional salience, and enhance health more than do material things, we have some reason to say that for the human world, nature gives priority to people and that nature puts people at the centre of things.

Evolutionary Roots of Acquisitiveness and Love of Possessions
If some 40 per cent of our traits are influenced by our genetic inheritance,[63] one might well search the record for the influence of that inheritance on, if not materialism, at least acquisitiveness. One

approach to evolutionary theory is through the behaviour of very young children. Lita Furby reviewed the evidence in the Human Relations Files and concluded: 'The large majority of references stated or implied that children are naturally possessive and acquisitive and that society must inculcate something different if so desired.' But she was sceptical: 'most of the material was too general and fragmented for solid conclusions.'[64] On the other hand, there are certain repeated and possibly universal experiences that might make the appreciation of 'what is mine' and what is not mine (yours, theirs) a universal culturally learned disposition.[65] In fact, children who are exceptionally acquisitive for material objects are distinguished by their poor linguistic and social development, a condition that tends to be fixed for the remainder of the child's life if not corrected by age six.[66] Healthy social development is marked by relatively low acquisitiveness.

Ernest Beaglehole searched for animal behaviour that might suggest acquisitiveness and found that, except for hoarding for nest-building and food, there was no evidence of cross-species acquisitiveness that matched the human pattern.[67] Similarly, laboratory experiments with animals show that they will do their work for 'pay' but they increase their work as pay is decreased — hardly a pay maximising behaviour.[68] In another approach, Lawrence Becker, a property lawyer, searched for the origins of individual possessiveness in territoriality, and was equally dismissive of any evolutionary foundations for human acquisitiveness and possessiveness. Among other points, Becker found that territoriality was a group and not an individual claim — territoriality worked through bonding.[69]

Human conspecifics, other people, are endowed by nature with powers of mutual attraction, emotional stimulation, and the very brain is organised for such responsiveness. Possessions are not similarly endowed; we allow desire for possessions to block our attraction to people at our peril. Although we may be required to break market 'laws' to reach the New Humanism, apparently we will do so with the support of our natural instincts.

I leave you with a puzzle. Advanced societies are now on the threshold of a New Humanism where persons and companionship can take the place of things and their acquisition. Markets have made us rich enough so that we can afford to follow a social rather than a materialist programme, apparently a programme closer to our natures. At long last we can afford to put human qualities and our preferences for other human beings at the centre of things. But the market economics that brought us here inhibits the exercise of these preferences, partly by requiring us, as a condition of our wealth, to place a high premium on money, and if we are to be happy at our work, to make this sacrifice gladly. Are we waiting for the bourgeoisie to fulfill Marx and Engels' famous prophecy? 'What the bourgeoisie . . . produces above all are its own gravediggers.'

And can one travel across a threshold in a paradox?

Notes

1.   Aristotle, *Nichomachean Ethics,* trans. J. A. K. Thomson; rev. H. Tredennick (Harmondsworth, UK: Penguin).

2.   Immanuel Kant, *Preface to the Fundamental Principles of the Metaphysic of Morals,* ed. and trans. T. K. Abbott, and published as *Kant's Theory of Ethics,* 6th ed. (London: Longmans, Green, 1920); reprinted in T. M. Greene, ed., *Kant Selections* (New York: Scribner's Sons), p. 37.

3.   Theodore W. Schultz. *Investing in People: The Economics of Population Quality* (Berkeley, CA: University of California Press, 1981), p. xi.

4.   Adam Smith (1776). *An Inquiry into the Nature and Causes of the Wealth of Nations,* ed. Edwin Cannan (New York: Modern Library/Random House, 1937), pp. 70–71.

5.   Frank M. Andrews and Stephen B. Withey, *Social Indicators of Well-Being: Americans' Perceptions of Life Quality* (New York: Plenum, 1976), pp. 306, 332.

6.   F. Thomas Juster. 'Preferences for Work and Leisure,' in *Time, Goods, and Well-Being,* eds. Juster and Frank P. Stafford (Ann Arbor, MI: Institute for Social Research, 1985), pp. 333–51.

7.   Ronald Inglehart, *Modernization and Postmodernization: Cultural, Economic, and Political Change in 43 Societies.* (Princeton: Princeton University Press, 1997), p. 101. But other studies of other kinds of materialism show only low correlations with education. Marsha L. Richins and Scott Dawson, 'A Consumer Values Orientation for Materialism and its Measurement: Scale Development and Validation,' *Journal of Consumer Research* 19 (1992), pp. 303–316 at 311.

8.   Angus Campbell, *The Sense of Well-Being in America* (New York: McGraw-Hill, 1981).

9.   Joseph Luft, 'Monetary Value and the Perception of Persons,' *Journal of Social Psychology* 46 (1957), pp. 245–251.

10.   But, since intrinsic work satisfaction may have increasing marginal utility, the same claim does not apply to work satisfaction. In general, skills have, for a period, increasing returns.

11.   Ruut Veenhoven, *Happiness in Nations: Subjective Appreciation of Life in 56 Nations 1946–1992* (Rotterdam: Erasmus

University, RISBO Press, 1993), pp. 50, 127. But see Ed Diener, Marissa Diener, and Carol Diener, 'Factors Predicting the Subjective Well-Being of Nations,' *Journal of Personality and Social Psychology* 69 (1995), pp. 851–864 at 861.

12. Ronald Inglehart and Jacques-Rene Rabier, 'Aspirations Adapt to Situations – But Why Are the Belgians so Much Happier than the French? A Cross-Cultural Analysis of the Subjective Quality of Life,' in *Research on the Quality of Life*, ed. Frank M. Andrews, (Ann Arbor, MI: Institute for Social Research, 1986), p. 46.

13. Ed Diener, private communication, 17 January 1995; Robert E. Lane, *The Loss of Happiness in Market Democracies* (New Haven: Yale University Press, 2000), p. 20.

14. Andrews and Withey, *Social Indicators of Well-Being*, p. 124; Angus Campbell, Philip E. Converse, and Willard L. Rodgers, *The Quality of American Life: Perceptions, Evaluations, and Satisfactions*, (New York: Russell Sage, 1976), p. 76.

15. Additional important contributions are made by 'things you do with your family' and, to a lesser degree, satisfaction with friends and 'the people you meet socially', Andrews and Withey, ibid., p. 124.

16. Lane. *The Loss of Happiness in Market Democracies*, pp. 99–124.

17. Diener, Diener, and Diener, 'Factors Predicting The Subjective Well-Being of Nations,' p. 657.

18. People are happier in individualistic countries, but when income is controlled, the relationship becomes only marginally significant (Diener, Diener, and Diener, pp. 858, 862).

19. Lane, *The Loss of Happiness in Market Democracies*, pp. 113–119.

20. Marsha L. Richins and Scott Dawson, 'A Consumer Values Orientation for Materialism and its Measurement: Scale Development and Validation,' *Journal of Consumer Research* (1992), pp. 303–316 at 308. Burkhard Strumpel finds that achievement orientation does not imply materialism. Burkhard Strumpel, ed., 'Economic Lifestyles, Values, and

Subjective Welfare,' in *Economic Means for Human Needs* (Ann Arbor, MI: Institute for Social Research), p. 41.

21.   Richins and Dawson, 'A Consumer Values Orientation for Materialism and Its Measurement Scale,' p. 313. All of the correlations mentioned in the text were at or less than p < .01.

22.   Tim Kasser and Richard M. Ryan, 'A Dark Side of the American Dream: Correlates of Financial Success as a Central Life Aspiration,' *Journal of Personality and Social Psychology* 65 (1993), 410–422 at 415–416. Tocqueville comments: 'It is strange to see with what feverish ardour the Americans pursue their own welfare, and to watch the vague dread that constantly torments them lest they should not have chosen the shortest path which may lead to it.' *Democracy in America*, Phillips Bradley, ed. (New York: Knopf), p. 136.

23.   H. W. Perkins, 'Religious Commitment, Yuppie Values, and Well-Being in Post-College Life,' *Review of Religious Research* 32 (1991), pp. 244–251. I am grateful to David Myers for this summary.

24.   Richins and Dawson, 'A Consumer Values Orientation for Materialism and Its Measurement Scale,' pp. 312–313.

25.   Tim Kasser and Richard Ryan, 'Further Examining the American Dream: Differential Correlates of Intrinsic and Extrinsic Goals,' *Personality and Social Psychology Bulletin* 22 (1996), pp. 280–287 at 283; Richins and Dawson, 'A Consumer Values Orientation for Materialism,' p. 311.

26 .   Kasser and Ryan, 'Further Examining the American Dream,' p. 285.

27.   E. L. Deci and R. M. Ryan, *Intrinsic Motivation and Self-Determination in Human Behavior,* (New York: Plenum, 1985).

28.   Mark R. Lepper and David Greene, eds., *The Hidden Costs of Rewards: New Perspectives on the Psychology of Human Motivation* (Hillsdale, NJ: Erlbaum, 1978). The argument has research support, but we should not forget that one of the reasons possessions are gratifying is that they enhance a sense of control. See Lita Furby, 'Possessions: Toward a Theory of Their Meaning and Function Throughout the Life Cycle,' in

Life-Span Development and Behaviour, ed. P. B. Baltes (New York: Academic Press, 1978), p. 322.

29. Edward E. Lawler, III, *Pay and Organizational Effectiveness* (New York: McGraw-Hill, 1971). Kasser and Ryan, 'A Dark Side of the American Dream,' pp. 415–416. The idea that working with things is less rewarding than working with ideas or people has received only moderate support. See Melvin L. Kohn and Carmi Schooler, *Work and Personality: An Inquiry into the Impact of Social Stratification* (Norwood, NJ: Ablex, 1983), p. 64.

30. 'The lust for goods can be *insatiable:* the pleasures of a new acquisition are quickly forgotten and replaced with a desire for more. This cycle leads inevitably to dissatisfaction and discontent. . . . Empirical tests using earlier measures of materialism support this hypothesis.' Richins and Dawson, 'A Consumer Values Orientation for Materialism and Its Measurement Scale,' p. 308. My emphasis.

31. M. Joseph Sirgy, 'Materialism and Quality of Life,' *Social Indicators Research* 43 (1998), pp. 227–260 at 228.

32. Harold Laski believed that Americans are notably 'troubled in their consciences' because of the conflict between their dominant materialism and the 'American dream of equal opportunity which is always challenging the values of a *business civilization'. The American Democracy* (New York: Viking, 1948), p. 12.

33. Daniel K. Yankelovich, *Changing Values in the 1970s: A Study of American Youth* (New York: John D. Rockefeller 3rd Fund,1974), p. 16; the same proportion of national samples of adults in Europe (1981 and 1990) agreed. Ashford and Timms, *What Europe Thinks,* pp. 134–136. Reports on the meaning of money also suggest conflict and ambivalence. Some accounts refer to the following money problems: obsession with money, anxiety about money, conflict between retentiveness (saving, niggardliness) and spending binges, distrust, shame, self-punishment, money as moral evil, and money as security. Robert E. Lane, 'Money Symbolism and Economic Rationality,' *The Market Experience* (New York: Cambridge University Press).

34. Jeremy Bentham commented: 'The desire for wealth is reproached, but desire for labour is the same thing and this is approved. Under another name, *the desire for wealth* has been furnished with a sort of letter of recommendation, which under its own name could not have been given to it.' *Jeremy Bentham's Economic Writings,* W. Stark, ed. (1954), vol. III. Royal Economic Society by George Allen & Unwin, 427.

35. Russell W. Belk, 'Three Scales to Measure Constructs Related to Materialism: Reliability, Validity, and Relationships to Measures of Happiness,' in *Advances in Consumer Research* 11, Thomas Kinnear, ed. (UT: Association for Consumer Research, 1983), pp. 291–297; and Russell W. Belk, 'Materialism: Trait Aspects of Living in a Material World,' *Journal of Consumer Research* 12 (1985), pp. 265–280.

36. Jane Loevinger, *Ego Development* (San Francisco: Jossey-Bass, 1976), p. 19. Maturity is here measured by indicators of ego-development where at a rather early 'conformist stage', people are concerned with 'social acceptance and reputation, and . . . *material things.*' (Emphasis added.) As a caveat, however, note the rejection of material values by youth in the 1960s occurred just at the time that a higher incidence of depression and increased unhappiness prevailed among the young.

37. Kasser and Ryan, 'A Dark Side of the American Dream,' p. 420; Richins and Dawson, 'A Consumer Values Orientation for Materialism and its Measurement', p. 303; Kasser and Ryan, 'Further Examining the American Dream,' p. 284.

38. Juster, 'Preferences for Work and Leisure,' p. 336.

39. Kasser and Ryan, 'Further Examining the American Dream,' p. 286; K. M. Sheldon and T. Kasser, 'Coherence and Congruence: Two Aspects of Personality Integration,' *Journal of Personality and Social Psychology* 68 (1995), pp. 531–543.

40. Karl Polanyi, 'Our Obsolete Market Mentality,' in *Primitive, Archaic and Modern Economies* (Boston: Beacon, 1995), p. 66.

41. 'In the postmodernisation phase of development, emphasis shifts from maximising economic gains – the central goal of modernization – to maximising subjective well-being.' Ronald Inglehart and Marita Carballo, 'Does Latin America Exist?

(And is There a Confucian Culture?): A Global Analysis of Cross-Cultural Differences', *PS: Political Science and Politics* XXX (1997), pp. 34–46 at 39.

42. John Maynard Keynes. 'Economic Possibilities for Our Grandchildren,' *Essays in Persuasion,* in *Collected Works of John Maynard Keynes,* vol. IX (London: Macmillan for the Royal Economic Society, 1972), pp. 321–334 at 329. Keynes went on to say 'All kinds of social customs and economic practices, affecting the distribution of wealth and economic rewards and penalties, which we now maintain at all costs, because they are tremendously useful in promoting the accumulation of capital, we shall then be free, at last, to discard.' What will happen to Keynes's discipline when acquisitiveness declines? Hirschman proposes that 'the main impact of *The Wealth of Nations* was to establish a powerful economic justification for the untrammeled pursuit of individual self-interest' – as contrasted to the previous political justifications. Albert O. Hirschman, *The Passions and the Interests: Political Arguments for Capitalism Before its Triumph* (Princeton: Princeton University Press, 1977), p. 100.

43. Eric L. Dey, Alexander W. Astin, and William S. Korn, *The American Freshmen: Twenty-Five Year Trends* (Los Angeles: Higher Education Research Institute, Graduate School of Education UCLA, 1991). Alexander Astin and others, *The American Freshmen: National Norms for Fall 1991* (and ensuing volumes through 1995) (Los Angeles: High Education Research Institute, UCLA, 1991–1995). The graph and citation are copied from a manuscript kindly sent to me by David Myers, Hope College. A confirming study that pinpoints the period of greatest change is offered by the pollster and savant, Daniel Yankelovich, who found an extraordinary shift toward goal materialism. Over the three years from 1970 to 1973, the students in his national college sample drastically shifted their concept of 'most important goals' to emphasise 'the money you earn' from 36% in 1970 to 61% in 1973. An account in the *New York Times* of 1 January 1987 gives a report of a similar survey of California freshmen:

over the decade 1976 to 1986, the proportion of freshmen reporting that it is important 'to promote racial understanding' declined from 36% to 27% while the proportion believing that it is important 'to be very well off financially' increased from 53% to 73%. (Yankelovich, *Changing Values* p. 16.) The evidence of a rise in materialist values among the young is overwhelming. For further evidence, see: Frank Levy, 'Happiness, Affluence, and Altruism in the Postwar Period', in *Horizontal Equity, Uncertainty, and Economic Well-Being*, Martin David and Timothy Smeeding, eds. (Chicago: University of Chicago Press, 1985), pp. 7–34.

44.   Inglehart, *Modernization and Postmodernization*, p. 112.

45.   Elinor Scarborough, 'Materialist-Postmaterialist Value Orientations,' in *The Impact of Values*, Jan W. van Deth and Elinor Scarborough, eds., vol. 4 of *Beliefs in Government*. (Oxford: Oxford University Press, 1995), pp. 123–159 at 138.

46.   Kasser and Ryan, 'A Dark Side of the American Dream,' p. 412.

47.   The trouble with this theory is that occupation is not closely linked to policy materialism in Europe (Scarborough, pp. 149, 150) or goal materialism in the US (at least it is not related to income or closely related to education). Kasser and Ryan, 'Further Examining the American Dream, p. 383; Richins and Dawson, 'A Consumer Values Orientation for Materialism and Its Measurement Scale,' p. 311.

48.   Inglehart and Rabier, 'Aspirations adapt to Situations,' p. 22.

49.   Strumpel, 'Economic Life-Styles, Values, and Subjective Welfare,' p. 27.

50.   Frank Knight, *The Ethics of Competition and Other Essays* (New York: Augustus Kelley, 1935), p. 44.

51.   Keynes, 'Economic Possibilities for Our Grandchildren,' p. 330–332.

52.   Friedrich Engels. n.d. c. 1933 [1890] *Socialism: Utopian and Scientific*. In V. Adoratsky, ed. *Karl Marx: Selected Works* (New York: International Publishers Press), pp. 185, 186.

53.   Inglehart, *Modernization and Postmodernization*, pp. 23, 27.

54. Ibid., p. 93.

55. Natalie Angier, 'What Makes a Parent Put up with it all?', *New York Times*, 2 November 1993, C1, p. 14.

56. Natalie Angier, 'Status Isn't Everything, at Least for Monkeys,' *New York Times*, 18 April 1995, C1.

57. John H. Flavell, 'Cognitive Development: Children's Knowledge About the Mind.' *Annual Review of Psychology* 50 (Palo Alto: Annual Reviews, 1999), pp. 21–45.

58. Hugh McIntosh, 'New Technologies Advance Study of Autism,' *APA Monitor* 29 (November 1998), p. 14.

59. While the sexes do not appear to differ appreciably on data versus ideas, they routinely differ by a full standard deviation on people versus things (females tend to gravitate toward the former, males toward the latter). David Lubinski, 'Scientific and Social Significance of Assessing Individual Differences: Sinking Shafts at a Few Critical Points,' *Annual Review of Psychology* 51 (2000), pp. 405–444 at 421.

60. David O. Sears, 'The Person-Positivity Bias,' *Journal of Personality and Social Psychology* 44 (1983), pp. 233–250 at 233.

61. Klaus R. Scherer, 'Emotion Experiences Across European Cultures: A Summary Statement,' in *Experiencing Emotion: A Cross-Cultural Study*, eds. Scherer, Harold L. Wallbott, and Angela B. Summerfield, Cambridge: Cambridge University Press, (1986), p. 176.

62. Diane G. Symbaluk, C. Donald Heth, Judy Cameron, and W. David Pierce, 'Social Modeling, Monetary Incentives, and Pain Endurance,' *Personality and Social Psychology Bulletin* 23 (1997), pp. 258–269.

63. For further discussion, see Lane, *The Market Experience*, pp. 563–568.

64. Furby, 'Possessions: Toward a Theory of Their Meaning and Function Throughout the Life Cycle,' pp. 304–305.

65. Somewhere Margaret Mead suggests that when toddlers begin to reach for things that do not belong to them, they are told 'that is not yours.'

66. Robert W. White, 'Exploring the Origins of Competence,' *APA Monitor* (April 1976), pp. 40–45.

67.   Ernest Beaglehole, *Property: A Study in Social Psychology* (London: Allen & Unwin, 1931).

68.   Stephen E. G. Lea, Roger M. Tarpy, and Paul Webley, *The Individual in the Economy* (Cambridge: Cambridge University Press, 1987), p. 165.

69.   Lawrence D. Becker, 'The Moral Basis of Property Rights,' in *Property,* NOMOS, vol. 22, eds. J. R. Pennock and J. W. Chapman, (New York: New York University Press, 1980), p. 201.

Why Are We Deaf to the Cry of the Earth?

Seán McDonagh, SSC

I will begin this talk with a quotation from Gerard Manly Hopkins's poem 'Binsey Poplars'. Though he lived at a time in the nineteenth century when there was a robust faith in the onward march of science and technology, he was acutely aware that uncontrolled technology could wreak havoc on other creatures and on the web of life. This sensitivity is obvious in 'Binsey Poplars'. He had come to know and love a strand of trees along a riverbank in Oxford. When he returned to the spot some time later he found the trees cut down and the place desolate.

Binsey Poplars (felled 1879)

My aspens dear, whose airy cages quelled,
Quelled or quenched in leaves the leaping sun,
    All felled felled, are all felled;
      Of a fresh and following folded rank
        Not spared, not one
        That dandled or sandalled
      Shadow that swam or sank
On Meadow and river and wind-wandering weed-winding bank.

O if we but knew what we do
    When we delve or hew-
Hack and rack the growing green!
Since country is so tender
To touch her being so slender,
That, like this sleek and seeing ball
But a prick will make no eye at all,
We, even where we mean

To mend her we end her,
When we hue and delve;
After-comers cannot guess the beauty been.
    Ten or twelve, only ten or twelve
    Strokes of havoc unselve
      The sweet especial scene,
    Rural scene, a rural scene,
    Sweet especial, rural scene.

Today the damage to the natural world is not confined to a single riverbank. During my twenty years as a missionary in the Philippines, I witnessed enormous destruction to the rainforest, mangrove forests, coral reefs, rivers, lakes and the soils of that country. A city like Manila was and is choking with air pollution and smog. It faces major problems supplying basic services like water and sanitation to its citizens in the coming years.

However, environmental damage is not confined to Third World countries. It is truly a global phenomenon and must be tackled as such by every human being and human institution. During my time in the Philippines I became involved in environmental issues. I worked with groups who were trying to protect what was left of the rainforest and, at the same time, replant in suitable places. I also began to encourage the Churches, particularly the Catholic Church, to become more pro-active in environmental matters though talks and writings.

Ending the Cenozoic Era

As we enter into the new millennium, all people are called to face the fact that our modern industrial society has taken a huge toll on the fabric of life of planet earth during the past one hundred years. The various industrial revolutions over the past two hundred years, from steam to the microchip, have delivered enormous benefits to about one fifth of humanity. This group includes the majority of people in First World countries and the elite in Third World countries. Many people are living longer, they are better fed and housed than any previous generation. We have access to choices, especially in the area of technology and medicine, that even kings couldn't dream of in the past.

But there is a dark side to these developments that I will reflect on in this talk. Put briefly, my thesis is as follows. We are destroying our air, water, and the life-giving quality of sunlight. We are poisoning our soils and causing the extinction of a vast number of creatures that God has placed on this earth with us. Every part of the globe and every ecosystem on earth has been affected. The damage everywhere is grave. In some situations it is irreversible. Unfortunately, church leaders of all traditions, in common with their counterparts in the educational, industrial, political and financial establishments, have been slow to understand the magnitude of the destruction.

Destroying the Earth

All that is possible in this presentation is to look at how crucial life-systems both globally and locally have already been damaged and how we might respond as Christians. In 1999 the executive director of the UN environment programme, Klaus Topfer, stated that the 'main threats to human survival were posed by water shortages, global warming and a new danger – worldwide nitrogen pollution.'[1]

The Greenhouse Effect

During the past two years, crude oil has gone from $10 to $35 a barrel. In Britain, hauliers protesting against the high price of fuel blockaded oil terminals and brought the country to a standstill. When the chancellor, Gordon Brown, with the backing of the Prime Minister, refused to cut taxes on diesel and petrol, the Labour Party's rating in the polls dropped precipitously. The truckers' action in Ireland on 15 September 2000 also called for a reduction in excise duty on diesel. The clear message is that the consumer wants cheap petrol no matter what the consequences. Unfortunately there was little strong, forceful leadership from politicians or religious leaders to address some of the ethical issues involved. Few were willing to mention the words 'environment' or 'greenhouse effect' in September.

The atmospheric concentration of carbon dioxide, methane, chloroflourocarbons (CFCs) and other 'greenhouse' gases are expected to increase by 30 percent during the next fifty years. This build-up is likely to increase the Earth's surface temperature by between 1.5 and 4.5 degrees centigrade by the year 2030. A study by a group of scientists in preparation for the international meeting on global warming in the Hague in November 2000 suggests that the 'upper range of warming over the next 100 years could be far higher than estimated in 1995'.[2]

Global warming will cause major, and in the main, deleterious climatic changes. In Northern latitudes, winters will probably be shorter and wetter, summers longer and drier. Sub-tropical areas might become drier and more arid while tropical ones might become wetter. The changes will have major, but as yet unpredictable, effects on agriculture and natural ecosystems.

As the oceans warm up and expand, sea levels will rise, leading to severe flooding over lowland areas. Unfortunately, the poorest countries, which emit very little greenhouses gases, will suffer most from climate change. Much of Bangladesh and the low-lying areas in many countries will simply disappear and create migration problems. According to *Time Magazine*, 4 September 2000, in Alaska melting permafrost has 'produced "roller coaster" roads, power lines tilted at crazy angles and houses sinking up to their window sashes as the ground liquefies'.[3]

Storms of great ferocity, like hurricane Mitch, which slammed into Central America in October 1998, the devastating floods and mudslides that killed over 10,000 on the Caribbean coast of Venezuela and the devastating wind storms that battered France after Christmas 1999 will probably become more frequent. As it surveyed the damage done by gales and flooding in southern England at the end of October 2000, the *Guardian* proclaimed in banner headlines: *Global Warming: It's With Us Now* (31 October 2000). According to Dr Mike Hulme of the University of East Anglia, Norwich, 'We are running massive risks by altering the climate of our planet in ways we do not fully understand, let alone are able to predict with confidence . . . . And the longer we continue to rely on a carbon-based energy economy, the greater the risks will be.'[4]

Recent studies predict that the global warming will not benefit Ireland and other countries in Northern Europe. An increase in temperature in the Arctic with the consequent melting of ice and release of fresh water into the Greenland Sea could interfere with the Gulf Stream and thus see a significant drop in temperature in Ireland, Britain and Norway.[5]

Kyoto

In the run-up to the United Nations meeting on climate change in Kyoto, Japan, in December 1997, a group of almost 2000 scientists comprising the Intergovernmental Panel on Climate Change (IPCC) called for a 60% reduction in the use of fossil fuel. Unfortunately, the politicians who attended the meeting in Kyoto, representing 160 countries, could only agree to a miserly 5.2% below 1990 levels by the year 2010. Despite these warnings, many countries, particularly the US, which is responsible for 23% of global warming, have made little progress towards implementing the Kyoto Protocol treaty. The US Senate has not ratified the treaty.

To date the Irish Government has not faced up to this global challenge, even though climate change will cause huge suffering for poor people. Ireland committed itself to limiting greenhouse gas emissions to 13% above 1990 levels by the year 2008–10. A report published by the Environmental Protection Agency in August 2000 entitled *Emissions of Atmospheric Pollutants in Ireland 1990–1998* claims that the greenhouse gas emissions for 1998 exceeded the limits agreed for the year 2010 under the Kyoto Protocol. According to Mr Michael McGettigan, a co-author of the report, 'Ireland faces the censure of other signatories to the Kyoto Protocol and a possible restriction on goods manufactured using processes that do not conform to the reduced-emissions policy'.[6] Greenhouse gas emission in Ireland rose by 18% between 1990–98.[7] Ireland may exceed its greenhouse gas target by a whopping 180% according to a front page story in the *Irish Independent,* 18 September 2000.

The Irish government needs to invest in and promote wind, water and wave power in order to move away from our over-dependence on fossil fuel. A levy on fossil fuel similar to the one being introduced by the Labour Government in Britain is urgently needed. This levy is not draconian and will only add 0.45p per unit to business energy bills. The levy will collect £1.1 billion per annum and this will be returned to industry through reductions that employers pay in National Insurance contributions for their employees.[8] The possibility of such a tax was contained in a Green Paper on energy published by the Department of Public Enterprise in September 1999.

Similar proposals for 'green taxes', especially on fossil fuel, were made by the EPA in April 2000. Little action has been taken to date, and the panic that gripped Western Europe about oil shortages in September makes it almost impossible to take effective action at Government level. Yet even a conservative and pro-business paper like the *Irish Independent* acknowledged in an editorial on 18 September 2000, that the 'government must make decisions, and it must face the fact that these may be highly unpopular decisions'.

One very important decision is to undertake a greenhouse audit on the £40 billion National Development Plan. The present plan, with its emphasis on a massive road-building programme, will only exacerbate an already terrible record in greenhouse gas emissions. The new emphasis should be on improving rail travel and making it more attractive and accessible to people. Calls for car-free days for cities or towns without good public transport and proper facilities for pedestrians and cyclists is hypocritical.[9]

On 2 November 2000 the Irish Government published a comprehensive plan to tackle Ireland's growing 'greenhouse' gas emissions in preparation for the meeting on global warming in the Hague. Among the initiatives mentioned, according to the *Irish Times,* are: unspecified tax on fossil fuel; closure or conversion of the Moneypoint coal-fired power station; reduction of the national herd to curb methane emissions; an option for industry to engage in carbon trading; encouragement to new householders to build more energy-efficient houses and tax support for more fuel-efficient cars.

Will the plan work? I have not seen the full text, but from what I have seen in the newspapers I am not too sure. Unless the goals are much more specific and the methodology and agents to implement the plan are much more clearly stated, I have my doubts. Voluntary efforts from industry in other areas, such as waste management, have proved ineffective. We still have not got a tax on plastic bags! There is no reason to think that it will be any different with energy consumption. Furthermore, if such a plan is to be successful it will need to be backed by a massive educational component and real support for alternative energy initiatives.

Two Locations in Ireland

A former Speaker of the House of Representatives in the US, Tip O'Neill, is reported to have said that all politics is local. Whatever about politics, all environments are local.

The Burren

Today I still find great joy in nature, especially in the Burren in County Clare. This area of Ireland, comprising about 150 square miles in North Clare and South Galway, has so many wonderful gifts. The sun shining on the limestone that was sculpted by a receding ice-sheet during the last ice age is a joy to behold. The mood on a wet day when overcast, leaden skies almost mingle with the grey of the limestone has its own appeal. At first sight the rocks seem barren, but a profusion of life lives in the clints and grykes that have been weathered by rainwater for aeons. On the hills one finds a diversity of plants, including spring gentians, mountain avens, burnet roses, carline thistles, heather, hairbells, O'Kelly's spotted-orchids, from regions as far apart as the Arctic and the Mediterranean. More than seven hundred different flowering plants and ferns have been found in the Burren. Twenty-eight of the thirty species of butterflies that are native to Ireland can be found in the Burren.

Mountains like Mullaghmore have a magical quality about them. Many of the 'green roads' offer spectacular views. I particularly like walking on a summer's day on the one in the north Burren above Black Head. The Burren, with its profusion of flowering plants, rises above on the right, with maybe a kestrel hovering around looking for its next meal, while the blue waters of Galway Bay and the Connemara hills stretch out to the left. Mystery also surrounds the numerous turloughs like the one at Carran. They fill up during the wet winter and retreat and almost disappear during a dry summer. Finally the underworld of caves, carved out over the millennia by underground streams has its own beauty and magic as any visitor to the Aillwee Caves can testify.

Thankfully, the visitor centre that the Office of Public Works (OPW) planned to build close to the Mullaghmore mountain will not go ahead. The argument has now been accepted that it is wrong to put a visitor centre in the middle of an area that is very sensitive ecologically. One risks destroying the beauty that draws people there in the first place.

Yet this beautiful habitat has being seriously ravaged in recent years, through changes in agriculture and the increased impact of tourism. Writing to the *Irish Times* on 19 May 2000, Dr Richard Moles of the Department of Chemical and Environmental Sciences at Limerick University complained that in recent years 'much has changed for the worse, and the rate of deterioration is increasing'. He complained that 'species-rich heathland (rare in this part [around Mullaghmore] of the Burren) had been trampled and over-grazed into species-poor grassland marred by bare soil scars, and the soil is being washed away into holes in the limestone. . . . Vegetation and soils are destroyed along tracks opened up by increasing number of hikers. Groves of aspen and other trees like birch and ash are unable to regenerate because of overgrazing by goats.'

In recent years I have seen fields of limestone being cleared and bulldozed, particularly east of Ballyvaughan. Instead of the variety of wildflowers that used to embellish the rock one now sees a thin layer of soil, planted with monotonous rye grass and the ubiquitous knapweed. One fears that it will only be a matter of time until holiday houses appear on this strip of land. As they say 'watch this space'!

It seems that foreigners are sometimes more aware of the destruction that is taking place in the Burren than Irish people. Writing to the *Irish Times* on 16 August 2000, Geraldine Exton from Frankston in Australia called attention to the fad among tourists to build their cairn in Poulnabrone and in the process disturb the fragile ecosystem.

Loss of Green Roads

I would like to see facilities put in place for people, Irish and tourists alike, to enjoy the Burren without destroying it. This is why I am particularly upset when the 'green roads' are interfered with and no longer accessible. In the area behind Fanore, the sign for the green road has disappeared and the field at the beginning of the road at Murroogh has been bulldozed. A newcomer, even with the aid of Tim Robinson's definitive map of the Burren, would find it difficult to locate the beginning of the road. At the Ballyvaughan side of that walk, the green road that Robinson shows leading down to the road does not, in fact, reach the highway.

Similarly the green road that used to pass through Gleninagh South has been encroached upon, so the right-of-way leading out over Gleninagh Pass is no longer available. Walking in Gleninagh in August this year, I noticed that Mr Jim Donoghue was seeking permission to construct eight holiday homes at Gleninagh South. On inspecting the planning application 9656 at the courthouse in Ennis, I was delighted to see that permission had been refused. If such holiday 'development' were allowed in the heart of the Burren, it would truly mean the end of the Burren as we know it.

My question, which echoes Dr Mole's concerns in the *Irish Times,* is as follows: Is anyone systematically monitoring the widespread changes that are now taking place in the Burren and responding to them in an appropriate way? Are Clare or Galway County Councils or Dúchas or other statutory bodies involved in the Burren capable of doing the job? I must say that I am very impressed with the work that has been initiated by Ms Congella Maguire, Heritage Officer for the Clare County Council. Through the programme 'Planning for Real', she and others are attempting to bring together many different interest groups and involve them directly in protecting their environment.

But is her remit wide enough? Will the programme be extensive enough and well enough funded? I am not sure. As an aside, the received wisdom, whether true or false, is that one of the reasons for Minister Síle De Valera's scepticism about Europe, which was reflected in her speech in Boston in September 2000, is that she was annoyed about the European Commission's role in promoting the Habitats Directive in the Burren.[10] All in all, Ireland's response to the environmental issue, be it in the area of water or waste management, is woefully inadequate. It would be much worse were it not for the fact that the EU is constantly encouraging and often badgering the Irish Government, often through threatening court action, to implement its environmental policies.

I propose that serious consideration be given to setting up a Burren Authority to effectively protect this special area of Ireland and promote it in appropriate ways. To make a difference, the agency would need to be well-funded financially, staffed by competent people and as free as possible from political interference. The staff ought to be drawn from a variety of backgrounds. This might range from a conservation perspective for the flowers, birds and habitat to agriculture, tourism and local government. To function effectively the agency would need to develop a good working relationship with local communities and various sectors within the community, and with the Department of Agriculture and Tourism. Such an agency located in a town or village in the Burren could bring a creative and imaginative approach to making the Burren a better place to live in and visit while protecting its beauty and uniqueness for future generations.

Kilkee

Kilkee, situated on the Atlantic ocean, is one of the best known resorts in the west of Ireland. The beautiful curve of the bay, Burn's Cove, the Pollock Holes, the Diamond rocks and the cliff walk all add their particular charms to this beautiful place. The history of Kilkee as a seaside resort goes back over two centuries. In 1793 the *Ennis Chronicle* advertised 'Kilkee House' as a suitable place for the bathing season.

A considerable amount of building took place in Kilkee before the Famine. Building continued in the second half of the nineteenth century in the McDonnell Estate at the west end and in the eastern side on lands that reverted to the Marquis of Conyngham in 1859. Conyngham had grandiose plans for buildings on the east side but with the exception of two model houses the plan did not come to fruition.

Recent Building Spree

During the past decade the feverish building programme driven by tax inducements, or more correctly called tax avoidance schemes, has totally transformed and deformed the face of Kilkee. I question whether the 'so-called' development during the past decade meets three fundamental principles of planning, namely that it should be *ecologically sustainable, socially just* and *architecturally appropriate*.

Housing Boom

The number of houses in Kilkee prior to 1990 was 595, of which 428 were occupied all year round. In other words 71.9 per cent of the housing stock was inhabited throughout the year. From 1992 to 2000 a total of 795 new houses were built in Kilkee. This represents an increase of 132.77%. Interestingly enough, the dramatic increase in houses has not lead to a massive increase in the permanent population. Most of the new buildings are holiday houses and are only occupied for a few months of the year. Those who occupy them have very little permanent engagement with the community. At the moment, only 34.25% of the housing in Kilkee is now inhabited all year round. Has anyone involved in the planning process researched what such a percentage drop in permanent residency will mean to a coastal town like Kilkee? I'd wager they have not.

Inadequate Sewage and Water Facilities
Despite this building spree, the infrastructures to support it by way of adequate sewage and water facilities have been woefully inadequate. Even as I speak, Kilkee is still dependent on the sewage system that was upgraded in 1973. Untreated sewage is discharged into the ocean west of the town in Intrinsic Bay. There is no definite plan to upgrade the present sewage system to meet the 2005 EU directive which demands that untreated sewage should not be discharged into the ocean. In a letter dated 12 September 2000, Clare County Council's County Engineer told me that 'In the Council's Assessment of Needs of February 2000, the provision of sewage treatment in Kilkee was prioritised at No. 5. Unfortunately, Kilkee did not feature in the recently announced Water Service Investment Programme.'[11]

The water system is also inadequate. During the summer months, residents of the Miltown Road and McSweeney Terrace complained about not being able to take a shower until after midnight due to insufficient water pressure. In some households filling a kettle is quite tedious and frustrating as the water trickles out. One household bought four washing machines in a period of four years. In recent years residents of Kilkee have had to install, at their own expense, extra water tanks so that they have access to a constant supply of water.

Looking at the building programme from a justice perspective, one could ask why was it not accompanied by a well-thought-out programme to provide basic civic facilities for the inhabitants of the town, especially the young and the elderly? There was no public provision for a park, for a sporting area where young people could kick a football, puck a *sliotar* or play basketball during the long summer evenings. St Joseph's Community College, the sole provider of secondary level education in the peninsula, has 335 students. The school has no gym, no hall, no track or playing pitch. The school teams, both boys and girls, often have to train on the strand. If it were not for the local GAA, who have a pitch outside the town, there would be no facilities for young people at all. One does not need to be a social worker to realise that the lack of adequate playing and recreation facilities can contribute to experimentation with drugs and alcohol among young people. The planning process seems to overlook these basic needs.

One final point on the social justice angle. In 1998 a holiday home on the Miltown Road cost £140,000. A small number of houses in the Moore Bay complex were advertised for local purchase at £78,000. How can a local young couple buy houses at such inflated prices? I do not know of any effective scheme either at the local, county or national level that is addressing an imbalance that in large part was created by government-sponsored tax breaks for the wealthy.

Looking at what has happened, one could be forgiven for thinking that the builders and planning authorities had only one idea in mind – to build as many houses as possible in every available piece of land. Some houses built with a view of the ocean in the mid '90s had this view completely obstructed by the next phase of the building programme. The only view from one house is up into the sky.

What About the Future?
Given the record of the past few years, my fear is that since every free spot in town has been built on, the planners will sanction a building programme for the most exclusive clients on the coast road leading out towards the Golleen. This is a sensitive habitat for choughs, or jackdaws. They need lands that are grazed and closely cropped by cattle or sheep. If the present habitat is destroyed and replaced by houses with lawns, this will mean the end of the chough population. But will that deter planners from sanctioning ribbon development along the road? If the past few years are anything to go by, the answer must be an emphatic no, especially since permission has been given to

go ahead with the golf course in Doonbeg. The only place left for exclusive houses is on the coast road. So unless things change dramatically it is farewell to the choughs.

Beach
Kilkee, with its large circular beach of firm sand and lack of currents, is an ideal spot for swimming, especially for young children. It is important for its tourist reputation that a seaside resort like Kilkee retains its prestigious Blue Flag status. The Blue Flag scheme is an initiative of the Foundation for Environmental Education in Europe (a network of twenty-two non-government organisations). In Ireland the scheme is administered by An Taisce with financial support from the Department of the Environment. To receive the Blue Flag, a beach must meet the criteria laid down in the EU Directive on Quality of Bathing Waters, and the Local Authority must ensure that adequate sanitary services and infrastructure are in place. The Local Authority must sample the water every two weeks during the bathing season for faecal bacteria and other pollutants.

Kilkee had a Blue Flag until 1995. It lost it between 1996 and 1998. The reason seems to be that at least one of the two streams flowing into the beach – the Victoria Stream or the Atlantic Stream – was polluted. In the summer of 1998, Clare County Council erected a sign stating: 'This stream and the immediate vicinity is at present unsuitable for bathing or paddling due to recent high levels of bacteria. Please swim in approved designated area as indicated by buoys and signage.' A hundred yards along the beach another sign read: 'Bathing Permitted'. At a public meeting called by the Planning Review Group in August 1998, the local GP told a packed hall that Clare County Council were obviously dealing with a very intelligent bacteria that would avoid floating away from where the sign said 'No Bathing'.

In 1999 and again in 2000 I noticed that the mouth of the Victoria Stream was blocked up when I visited in June, July and August. Once in 1999, after a flood, the waters burst through the dam. In September 1999 and again in September 2000, the 12th to be exact, the 'dam' was removed and the stream was allowed to flow freely through the strand out to the sea. My question is: What is the purpose of this 'dam'? Is it a way of dealing with the fact that the Victoria Stream is polluted? Is it about retaining the Blue Flag? On 19 September I wrote to the Deputy County Manager raising these questions. The reply, dated 9 October 2000, stated that:

> The seasonal impoundment of the Victoria Stream outfall is easily explained as follows. The bathing water on Kilkee Beach has always and continues to meet EU Bathing Water Standards. The interpretation of these standards has, however, been such that individual discharges to beaches are required to meet the same standards. Most analysts will agree that it is virtually impossible to identify a stream which drains a typical urban and rural catchment which would have a water quality such that it meets the Bathing Water Requirements. While I fear that this requirement is somewhat unfair, I do acknowledge that there is an intrinsic attraction for children to play in such streams which flow across beaches used for amenity purposes. Accordingly, practical and pragmatic solution has been to divert the low flows in the stream to the pumping station during the bathing season.

As you can well imagine, I was not happy with this response and emailed a number of questions in reply. I believe that it would be better to deal with the pollution at sources rather than this clumsy end of pipe solution. A model for dealing with water pollution at source can be found in the Lough Derg and Lough Ree Management Group Report. This study set out to 'identify river stretches (throughout the whole Shannon Catchment area) experiencing the effects of pollution, to catalogue the principal cause in each instance and to propose a range of key management measures which may be implemented by individual Local Authorities in problem areas'.[12]

I propose that Clare County Council ought to use this methodology in addressing pollution in both the Atlantic and Victoria Streams instead of the end-of-pipe solution that is presently in place. Such an approach would also be much better for the health of those who use the beach and swim in Kilkee.[13]

Why Are We So Insensitive to the Environment?

- We often fail to present an adequate context for understanding environmental issues. The most important thing when looking at the details of environmental devastation is to present it in an adequate context of understanding so that the implications of the data can be clearly appreciated. Unless this happens, it is very easy to fall into what I call the litany approach to the environment. This merely lists environmental problems and adds them to a host of other woes, such as poor housing, unemployment, immigration, social tension, etc.

- Such an approach trivialises the environmental issue for two reasons; Firstly, each new report of environmental damage is seen in isolation and thus the cumulative and global impact of what is happening can easily be missed. Looked at merely on a case by case basis, we can delude ourselves into thinking that ecological destruction is not a serious threat to life and that environmental campaigners are like the boy in the wolf story, simply trying to attract attention when there is no real danger.

    Secondly, there is usually a time lag between environmentally destructive activity, such as burning fossil fuel, and the moment when the resultant climate change is evident. No sane person will jump from a five-story building and hope to survive; the consequence of such a foolish action is clear and immediate. This, however, is not true in the domain of environmental problems like global warming, acid rain, ozone depletion, or mercury poisoning. It may be decades before the impact of our actions today, on the earth and human community, is truly appreciated. Since our industrial society is focused on immediate gratification, this time lag permits politicians and communities to leave environmental issues to one side, or to address them through fine rhetoric, while resources are concentrated instead on tangible problems, like unemployment, industrial growth or inflation. In fact, some of the accepted responses to today's problems, like promoting economic growth as a way of dealing with unemployment, can increase environmental damage in the long run, and thus preclude the possibility for really good human work in a locality for decades or even centuries.

- In Ireland we are poorly served by the media when it comes to educating the public about the importance of environmental concerns. There is no environmental programme on RTÉ – Television or Radio. When I came home from the Philippines in the early 1990s there were two programmes I listened to on Saturday mornings – *Scrap Saturday*, followed by an environment programme. There was a hue and cry when *Scrap Saturday* was scrapped. There was no agitation when the environment programme was dropped. Radio One has *Mooney Goes Wild on One* on Sunday mornings. I listen to it as often as I can, but it is a naturalist, or natural history programme rather than an environment programme.
- On the print media side things are even worse. The environment is usually treated as a news item. All Irish newspapers have supplements on sport, finance, property, farming, etc. The only paper on these islands that has a regular environment section is the *Guardian*.
- On the political front, the most important development in recent years has been the establishment of the Environmental Protection Agency (EPA) on 26 July 1993. The Agency has a wide range of statutory duties and powers under law. The non-governmental organisation (NGO) community at the time, while welcoming the establishment of the EPA, was concerned about whether it would be properly funded and also felt that an agency that grants licences to industries to pollute (which is what IPCC licences are) should not be monitoring compliance; a separate agency should have that responsibility. It would be like asking the Dáil deputies who make the laws to become the judges in their own constituencies.
- Concern for the environment is not high on the priority list of any political party apart from the Greens. It is true that legislation is often passed, but then it is not implemented. According to the Wildlife Act (1976, amended in 1999) it is an offence to cut hedges between 1 April and 31 August. How many times did each one of you see hedges being cut for County Councils between those dates this year? Needless to say no prosecution has been taken under the Wildlife Act.
- In April 1997 Fianna Fail published a document on genetically engineered organisms, in which Joe Walsh and Noel Dempsey, then opposition spokespersons for Agriculture and the

Environment, stated that 'it is premature to release genetically modified organisms into the environment or to market food which contains genetically modified ingredients . . .' The reason for such a stand was that 'Fianna Fail will not support what amounts to the largest nutritional experiment in history with the consumer as the guinea pig'. Immediately on entering government, Fianna Fail did a U-turn on that commitment and failed to inform the electorate why such a policy change was necessary. No wonder people are cynical about political commitments on environmental issues.

- We lack a basic ethical framework that would heighten our awareness about environmental destruction. Aristotle, whose impact on Western thought is enormous, held that since 'nature makes nothing without some end in view, nothing to no purpose. It must be that nature has been made for the sake of man.' This idea that animals and plants are created by God for humankind has dominated western attitudes towards the rest of creation for centuries.[14] Elements of the Judaeo-Christian tradition have strongly reinforced the Aristotelian legacy. Take the Genesis 1:26-28 text, 'Increase and multiply and dominate the earth.' This text has often been interpreted, mistakenly according to contemporary Scripture scholars, as giving humans a licence to dominate the earth and do whatever they wish with animals and plants.

- It is true that within the Judaeo-Chistian tradition there has been a strand that saw humans as stewards of Creation (Gen 2:15). Unfortunately, as the historian Clive Ponting points out in his *Green History of the World,* 'although the idea that humans have a responsibility to preserve the natural world of which they are merely guardians can be traced through a succession of thinkers it has remained a minority tradition. Unfortunately, St Francis's kinship with Brother Sun, Sister Moon and the rest of creation was a minority position. It did not inform western approaches to nature during the rise of modern science and the technologies that have flowed from scientific discoveries.

- There is very little appreciation that this generation has obligations to future generations. The challenges of inter-generational justice are seldom discussed. As a people we seem to be very insensitive to the environmental maxim that 'we do not inherit the earth, we borrow it from our children'.

- We should not overlook human greed and selfishness as an important element in the destruction of nature. Greed, in the sense of an intense selfish desire for money and material goods, is virtually synonymous with the sin of avarice as presented in the New Testament. As such it has been condemned in Catholic social teaching as the motivating force for economic behaviour. In Catholic social thought, the needs of the common good have always taken precedence over unreasonable individual self-interest. The numerous tribunals underway at the moment are a testimony to the fact that greed, rather than public service, has motivated a number of people in public life in Ireland in recent years.

How the Churches Might Respond to Environmental Ruin

Given that the Christian Churches have arrived at these challenges a little breathless and a little late, they must now make up for lost time and, in co-operation with other faiths, throw all their energies into urgently addressing the challenge of Justice, Peace and the Integrity of Creation. Unless this awareness is gained in the very near future, human beings and the rest of the planet's community will be condemned to live amid the ruins of the natural world.

The first and most important contribution that the churches could make to the present ecological crisis would be to acknowledge the magnitude of the problem and urge people to face it with courage.

Need for a Prophetic Witness from the Churches

Many Northern governments, and especially transnational corporations who have benefited from the current shape of the global economy, are unwilling to acknowledge the extent of the problem and as a consequence change their ways. As we saw earlier, the 2,000 scientists of the Intergovernmental Panel on Climate Change (IPCC) called for a 60% cut in emissions of greenhouse gases in an effort to lessen the full impact of global warming. Corporate interests, especially in the coal, oil and automobile sectors, have lobbied very effectively to block any increase in taxes on fossil fuel or any serious effort to reduce greenhouse gas emissions.

In the face of these efforts to downplay the seriousness of the climate change issue, the Churches must be resolute in their determination to witness to the truth. To date, the Churches have often taken a so-called 'balanced' position or have remained silent on ecological issues in order not to fall out with those who wield economic or political power. Such even-handedness is difficult to square with the gospel calls for a clear stance on the side of the poor and the exploited earth. This is the heart of the Church's prophetic responsibility.

The World Council of Churches has responded to this crisis by publishing a very thorough analysis of the ecological, economic, ethical, theological and pastoral aspect of global warming in a document called *Accelerated Climate Change: Sign of Peril, Test of Faith*.[15] The text discussed the theological and ethical issues involved in global warming and attempted to motivate the churches to become involved in the issue. All the Christian churches should throw their moral authority behind this document. It is worth remembering that while church presence was very evident at the United Nations conference on population in Cairo (1995), there was hardly a word from religious leaders before, during or since the Kyoto Protocol (December 1997), despite the fact that global warming will create misery for tens of millions of people.

Recently I was listening to a talk given by the Malaysian scholar Dr Chandra Muzaffar. While addressing the role of religion today in Asia, he made a point that I believe is applicable in Ireland. He stated that 'worship of wealth and the power and prestige it generates has become so pervasive that we can perhaps talk of 'moneytheism' as a formidable challenge to monotheism. Moneytheism, the ideology which legitimises the relentless pursuit of riches as an end in itself is the driving force behind the global economy. This global economy has sanctified the maximisation of profits as a planetary credo. The media, through advertisements, glorifies the opulent lifestyles that wealth can buy. Culture, politics, social life, all reflect, directly or indirectly, the overwhelming power of the ideology of moneytheism.'[16] He believes that all the major religions should avoid slipping into pietism or fundamentalism and function instead to critique and challenge this ideology, which is creating such cultural dislocation, social injustice and ecological devastation across the globe.

Toward a Theology and Spirituality of Creation

Another important contribution that the Churches can make is to develop a spirituality of creation. In attempting to do this, Christian thinkers will find many helpful insights both in the Biblical tradition and in different Christian spiritualities that have flourished, often, it must be admitted, at the margins, during the past two millennia. One thinks of the centrality of creation in both Celtic spirituality and the spirituality of St Francis of Assisi.

If this theology is to focus on the well-being of the total biosphere, or, in theological terms, on all God's creation, then it will have to adopt what the Australian biblical theologian, Elaine Wainwright, has called a 'hermeneutics of reclamation', simply because much of the classical Christian tradition is very human centred.[17] Genesis calls us to imitate a gracious God who loves Creation and cares for the Earth. One could begin 'this hermeneutic of reclamation' right at the first line of Genesis. The Bible affirms that the world was created by a personal God who declares that it is good and loves his creation (Gen. 1:1). This is an extremely important statement, as many cultures in the ancient Near East believed that, since the Earth was subject to decay, it must have been created, at least, in part, by an evil spirit. This belief still lingers on, even in the minds of people who profess to be Christian. It is one of the reasons why people who claim to be Christians can lay waste a forest or destroy fragile ecosystems without having the slightest twinge of conscience that what they are doing might be wrong.

Nature Has Value

In the Psalms (e.g., Ps 104) and Wisdom literature, especially the Book of Job, there is a clear appreciation that the *raison d'être* of creation is not found primarily in its ability to meet human needs. Creation has intrinsic value because it is created by God and sustained by God's Spirit. Furthermore, there is a strong sense of the interdependence of all creatures in Psalm 104. Ian Bradley in *God is Green* writes that, in the Bible, 'God is seen as the Lord of all creation and that 'there is a strong sense of the interdependence of all creatures and an image of the world as of a single cosmic community rather than (as) a collection of autonomous entities'.[18] I have come that they may have life and have it to the full (Jn 10:10).

A Christian theology of creation begins with the reality of the incarnation. This affirms that God became not merely a human being but a part of all creation. One difficulty with the theology of the incarnation almost from the beginning was that it tended to emphasise the divinity of Christ rather than his humanity. As a consequence, many patristic authors taught that God became human to make humans divine, 'not to celebrate but to overcome the frailties of the flesh that tied it to corruptibility and death'.[19]

Even a cursory reading of the Gospels reveal that Christians have much to learn from the attitude of respect that Jesus displayed towards the natural world. He enjoyed an intimacy with nature, which is evident from his parables – the sower and the seed (Mt 13:4-9, 18-23), the vine and the branches (Jn 15:1-17, Mk 12:1-12). He illustrated his stories by referring to the lilies of the field (Lk 12:27), the birds of the air (Mt 6:26) and foxes and their lairs (Lk 9:58).

In this age of unbridled consumerism, where greed is often represented as a virtue, it is important to remember that Jesus lived lightly on the Earth. He warned his disciples against hoarding possessions and allowing their hearts to be enticed by the lure of wealth (Mt 6:19-21). It is clear that we will find no support in the teachings of Jesus for the modern throw-away, earth-destroying consumer society.

Jesus as the Word and Wisdom of God is active before the dawn of time, bringing creation to birth out of the chaos. Through him the Universe, the Earth, and all life was created (Jn 1:3-5). All the rich unfolding of the universe – from the initial glow of the fireball, through the shaping of the stars and the earth as the green planet of the universe, right up to the emergence of humans and their varied cultures and histories – are centred on Jesus (Col 1, 16-17).

A number of theologians in recent years have attempted to shape a Trinitarian theology in the light of modern science and the ecological crisis. They argue that the most fruitful way of understanding the Divine today is to see the Divine reality as one of mutual and equal relations. 'If God is Being-in-Relation, then this provides a basis for thinking about reality as radically relational. A relational ontology provides a meeting point for Christian theology and evolutionary biology. In Christian theology, the relational Trinitarian God can be understood as making space with the divine relations for a dynamically unfolding universe and for the evolution of life in all its diversity and interconnectedness'.[20] Creation, then, is now understood as a community of beings interconnected with each other and with the triune God. Our way of relating within such an interdependent world must be through mechanisms or *koinonia* (community), rather than through dominant or exploitative behaviour.

An Earth Spirituality

The Bible vigorously denies that the world is evil. In chapter one of Genesis, God repeatedly contemplates what he has created and 'sees that it is good' (Gen 1:10, 18, 19, 21a and 26). It also affirms that the God whom we experience in our lives is not hiding in some inaccessible part of the Universe; Creation is alive with the presence of God if, like the Psalmist, we look at it through the eyes of Faith:

> The heavens are telling the glory of God;
> And the firmament proclaims his handiwork.
> Day-to-day pours forth speech,
> And night to night declares knowledge (Ps 19, 1-2).

I believe an authentic Creation spirituality would help regenerate Irish Christianity, and especially Irish Catholicism. Celtic spirituality celebrated the goodness of God that was manifest in the beauty of the world around us. Many Celtic monasteries were sited in remote and beautiful places like Skellig and Iona. It is no wonder that the monks came to love the cry of the curlew, the flight of the gannet, the bark of seals, the beauty of trees and wild flowers, and the buzzing of bees and insects. Such a spirituality has much wisdom to offer to modern Ireland. It reminds us that we do not have a right to dominate and exploit nature without a thought for the consequence for other creatures and future generations.

Many Irish poets point in a similar direction. Patrick Kavanagh's poem 'The One' is a case in point:

> Green, blue, yellow and red –
> God is down in the swamps and marshes
> Sensational as April and almost incredible the flowering of our
> catharsis.
> A humble scene in a backward place
> Where no one important ever looked
> The raving flower looked up in the face
> Of the One and the Endless, the Mind that baulked
> The profoundest of mortals. A primrose, a violet,
> A violent wild iris – but mostly the anonymous performers
> Yet an important occasion as the Muse at her toilet
> Prepared to inform the local farmers
> That beautiful, beautiful, beautiful God
> Was breathing His love by a cut-away bog.

Renewing Liturgy and Devotions

The Church should recognise the transformative power that liturgy and worship have in shaping individual and community values in a way that will promote justice and the integrity of creation. Good ritual can help communities evolve a new mode of human interaction with other human beings and with the natural world. Since the emergence of humankind on earth, people have always sought to link the deepest mysteries of their own personal and community life with the rhythms of the earth and cosmos through myths, rituals and ceremonies.

Sacraments

The sacramental liturgy of the Church offers many moments in which the Christian community can experience the presence of God in the world of nature. In the Catholic liturgy we are incorporated into the Church through the sacrament of baptism. The symbolism of baptism revolves around life-giving water and the power of the Spirit to transform the lives of individuals and whole communities. These ought to act as a strong incentive for the Christian community to ensure that their water and the waters in their locality are not polluted with toxic, human, industrial and agricultural waste. Baptism initiates people into the Christian community. But I feel that at this point in human and planetary history, we must expand the boundaries of what we understand as our community to include all the community of the living. It would be helpful if, in administering the sacrament of baptism, we saw it as not merely initiating people into the Catholic Church, but as initiating them also into the wider earth and cosmic community.

Eucharist

The Eucharist is also pregnant with all kinds of creative possibilities for deepening our awareness of the holy communion, which unites God, humankind, other creatures and all creation. In the Eucharist the elements of bread and wine, taken from the Earth and transformed by human labour, are offered in the memory of the Passion, Death and Resurrection of Jesus, and through the action of the Spirit they are transformed into the Body and Blood of Christ. The experience of Eucharist is a spur to Christians to work for a just, compassionate, sharing society. It also summons Christians to work for a sustainable society where seeds and soils are protected and the bonds of interdependence between humans and the rest of creation are more clearly understood and experienced. The Eucharist is that holy communion in which all the members give themselves to one another in order to promote abundant life for all.

Promoting and Preparing for a New, Sustainable Culture

Moving beyond liturgy, environmental issues must become part of the wider pastoral ministry of the Church. It is sad and ironic that the present ecological crisis is the result of considerable human success. Everyone will admit that greed, covetousness and other commonly recognised human vices have undoubtedly contributed to our present crisis. Nevertheless, the principal cause of ecological devastation in our world today has been the unrelenting pursuit of what many people consider a good and desirable thing – the modern, growth-oriented, industrial model of development. What many people feel is the good life, something to be aspired to and worked for, is in fact destroying the world.

On a local level, the economic boom in Ireland since the mid-1990s, with GDP growth rates of between 6 and 9 per cent, has taken a huge toll on the environment. Even the former Taoiseach, Dr Garret Fitzgerald, whose interests lie more in the economic field than the ecological one, believes that 'the Celtic Tiger threatens to devour Ireland's much-hyped pristine environment' (*Irish Times*, 26 May 1997).

The Churches must work assiduously with all those who are attempting to oppose this destructive way of living and espouse a more compassionate and sustainable culture that will support and enhance all life. The Dominican Sisters ought to be commended for not selling seventy acres of prime land in the vicinity of Wicklow. Instead they have transformed it into a biodynamic enterprise with a wildlife sanctuary and an ecology centre.[21] It would be a wonderful millennial initiative if other religious orders who still own land followed this creative example.

To date only one Irish bishop, Bishop Bill Murphy of Kerry, has tackled the environmental issue in a pastoral letter.[22] Given the environmental challenge globally and nationally, the fact that the leadership of the Irish Church has not addressed its moral and religious implications is in my mind a major failure in terms of effective episcopal leadership.

The Irish Bishops could perform a great service for both the Irish people and the environment by initiating a national dialogue about the environment. This process ought to be carried out on an ecumenical basis.

The Call to Renew the Earth

The ecological crisis is a moment of real challenge for our contemporary culture. Unless positive choices are made now, irreversible damage will be done to the Earth's fabric. Responding to the challenge will demand concrete choices for individuals and institutions to help bring about this new age. The Church, which Vatican II sees 'as a sign raised up among the nations' should be in the forefront in trying to usher in this new, ecological age where a mutually enhancing relationship ought to exist between humankind and the rest of creation.

Christians should also support environmental non-government organisations who are trying to raise awareness about ecological issues and campaign for change.

Let me end on a hopeful note. On the Feast of Pentecost we can call on the Holy Spirit: 'Come, O Holy Spirit fill the hearts of your faithful and enkindle in them the fire of your love. Send forth your spirit and they shall be created and you will renew the face of the Earth.' That is our challenge and our prayer. We know that the God who created and sustains this beautiful world mourns the destruction that is taking place in our time and that He/She is calling all of us in our own way to dedicate ourselves to healing and caring for the Earth. The worldwide growth of the ecological movement in recent years is a sign, to quote Gerard Manly Hopkins' poem 'Binsey Poplars' again:

> And for all this, nature is never spent;
> There lives the dearest freshness deep down things;
> And though the last lights off the black West went
> Oh, morning, at the brown brink eastwards, springs-
> Because the Holy Ghost over the bent
> World broods with warm breast and with ah! Bright wings.

Notes

1. Paul Brown, 'The Dilemma That Confronts the World,' *Guardian,* 16 September 1999, p. 3.

2. John Vidal, 'Global Warming is Greater than Predicted Study,' *Irish Times,* 27 October 2000.

3. Eugene Liden Churchill, 'The Big Meltdown,' *Time,* 4 September 2000.

4. Dr Mick Hulme, 'There is no longer such a thing as a purely natural weather event,' *Guardian,* 15 March 2000, p. 4.

5. Tim Radford, 'Melting Arctic Will Mean Chillier Britain,' *Guardian,* 7 April 2000, p. 9. Also Dick Ahlstrom, 'Climate Change May Switch Off the Gulf Stream,' *Irish Times,* 2 November 2000, p. 16.

6. Tim O'Brien, 'State Faces Penalties Over Greenhouse Gas Emissions,' *Irish Times,* 26 August 2000, p. 5.

7. Tracy Hogan, 'Greenhouse Gases Head for Twice Agreed Levels,' *Irish Independent,* 28 April 2000, p. 10.

8. Polly Toynbee, 'Going Up in Smoke', *Guardian,* 1 September 2000, p. 15.

9. Tracy Hogan and Kathy Donaghy, 'Car-Free Days a Recipe for Traffic Chaos, Says AA,' *Irish Independent,* 30 August 2000.

10. Patrick Smith, 'Was Síle Thinking of EU Curbs on Burren Changes?' *Irish Times,* 26 September 2000, p. 16.

11. A member of Clare County Council addressed this point after the conference, in a letter dated 24 November: 'Clare County Council prepared an Assessment of Needs in the Water Services Area last year and towards the end of the year, a priority list was adopted by the elected members. In this priority list, the provision of a new waste water treatment plant and an upgrade of the network features at No. 5. The four schemes having a higher priority than Kilkee have been included by the Minister in June of this year. For some time, Clare County Council has sought the approval of the Department of the Environment to a Brief which we prepared regarding the appointment of Consulting Engineers for the Scheme. I would have to be optimistic that progress will be made sooner rather than later.'

12. Lough Derg and Lough Ree Catchment Monitoring and Management System', Consultant Kirk McClure Norton, 40 Upper Canal Street, Dublin.

13. Clare County Council addressed this point after the conference, in a letter dated 24 Noevmber 2000: 'Any signage which was erected in Kilkee notifying the public of bacteriological contamination referred to stream flows meandering across the beach. I will respond to your allegation that my comments were both vague and unhelpful by advising that an EPA Biologist shares my view that it would be difficult to identify a stream whose quality meets Bathing Water criteria. This is mentioned in a report of a biological assessment of the Victoria Stream. From a common sense viewpoint, could I remind you that when you and I were growing up, farming practices were radically different, e.g. cattle bedded on absorbent straw producing a wonderfully usable dung fertiliser – compare this to intensive livestock rearing in slatted houses and consequent environmental loadings. Despite significant progress in combating pollution from agricultural sources, there is a continuing problem and I honestly believe from my own observations that it would be very difficult, regrettably, to find a pristine stream or watercourse. Of course, there are difficulties also with pollution of human origin. These include contamination arising from septic tank overflows in the rural part of the Victoria and Atlantic Stream Catchments. To a lesser extent, some contamination arises from contamination of surface water drains in the town by foul sewage. Historically a number of connections seem to have been inadvertently made to the stormwater system but this has been rectified through a painstaking investigation by Clare County Council followed by rectfication in all cases. You commented favourably on the Derg/Ree Project, which Clare County Council leads. In fact, Clare County Council has carried out extensive investigations on both Kilkee Catchments and this work is continuing. For your information, the provisions of the Water Pollution Act have been applied through notices and proceedings.'

14. Aristotle, *Politics* (Harmondsworth: Penguin, 1985).

15. *Signs of Peril, Test of Faith: Accelerated Climate Change,* World Council of Churches, 150, route de Ferney, PO Box 2100, 1221 Geneva 2, Switzerland, May 1994.

16. Dr Chandra Muzaffar, 'Religion in 21st Century Asia: A Challenge Without, A Change Within,' Melbourne, 23 October 2000.

17. Elaine Wainwright, 'A Metaphorical Walk through Scripture in an Ecological Age,' *Pacifica* (Summer 1994), PO Box 271, Brunswick East, Victoria 3057, Australia.

18. Bradley, Ian, *God is Green* (London: Longman, Darton and Todd, 1992), p. 19.

19. Rosemary Radford Ruether, 'Sex and the Body in the Catholic Tradition,' *Conscience* (A Newsjournal of Prochoice Catholic Opinion) (Winter 1999/2000), quoting Athanasius, *On the Incarnation of the Word Religious Tract Society* (London, 1903).

20. Ibid., p. 126.

21. Eilis Ryan 'Saving the Earth,' *Farmers Journal,* 15 May 1999, p. 3.

22. Bishop Bill Murphy, 'Going to the Father's House: A Jubilee People.' Pastoral Letter to the Diocese of Kerry 1999.

'IT'S JUST THE MEDIA!'

Colum Kenny

The relationship between citizens and the media needs to be redefined urgently. This is so not least because so much of our experience is filtered through the media. It is a process that begs questions about control and ownership and about the manner in which the media influences our identity as individuals or as a society. Because the media is so pervasive, we need to deepen our understanding of its complexity. The churches and educators have a role to play in fostering debates on media policy and practice.

At times, the complexity of issues may depress us. So in the face of global forces shaping our natural and social environments, it is important to recall the old Russian proverb, 'One work of truth can outweigh the whole world'. As my friend, the late Fr James McDyer of Glencolumbcille, liked to say, 'Better to light one candle than forever curse the darkness'. One way to light a candle is by articulating the truth in the face of confusion or exploitation.

As well as individuals answering back the media, it is desirable that governments and regulators across Europe take more seriously their democratic responsibilities in order to ensure high standards in broadcasting, especially, and that they co-operate more closely in monitoring and controlling certain trends in respect of the ownership and content of entertainment and media services.

Closer to home, I would like to see the Irish government implementing some of the recommendations of the Commission on the Newspaper Industry so that Irish newspapers may move as soon as possible to appoint an independent press complaints commission. I shall also raise the possibility of a system of self-regulation by broadcasters to replace the present Broadcasting Complaints Commission.

In all of this I am speaking from a position that takes for granted the desirability of freedom of speech. The redefinition of relationships between citizens and the media advocated here would actually strengthen our freedoms by protecting the individual against abuse by the rich or powerful. It can also protect journalists against commercial pressures that tempt them to lower their standards.

All of which having been said, or about to be said, it is worth recalling how Alfred Hitchcock used to respond to those critics who analysed any of his films too intently. He reminded them that it was 'only a movie'. In other words, people have a great capacity for both enjoying and seeing through artifice. However, that capacity is greatly challenged by the sophistication of modern media and of the related entertainment industry.

The media has increasingly *become* culture for many people. If an event is not in the papers or on the radio, TV or worldwide web, then to all intents and purpose it has not happened for the public. The media shapes our agenda, indicating to us what matters and, by its omission, what does not. What people discuss is so often what is discussed by the media. Public meetings have declined in frequency and importance as debates occur second-hand, with citizens reducing themselves to absent observers of carefully structured interviews or panel-talks that take place in distant locations. Afterwards, citizens may share their opinions about what they have read, heard or seen at a distance.

Politics, art, music, fashion – formative opinions on these and on other aspects of our cultural life reach most people through the media. Not only public debates but exhibitions, concerts, expressions of design and taste are all likely to be encountered or understood primarily through some newspaper or the pages of a magazine or a radio talk-show or the television screen. This is not necessarily a bad thing, but it does illustrate the potential power of media. The amount of time that people spend watching television on any one day is immense.

A. C. Nielsen, the reliable industry source of data on TV viewing, reports that the average adult in the Republic of Ireland spends 3.1 hours every single day watching television, while each Irish child watches 2.6 hours of television daily. That estimate does not include additional time spent watching videos, playing games on consoles or using the Internet. Then there's the radio, to which almost 90 per cent of us tune in to every day for a remarkable average time of over four hours each, or 235 minutes (Source RTÉ/JNLR, age 15+). We also continue to devour newspapers and magazines in large numbers. Such cold statistics paint a hot picture of the average Irish citizen as being someone who for much of their waking time (over seven hours daily) is wired to the electronic media, from which they take breaks to dip into the ink on printed pages.

This is a phenomenon that gives rise to some interesting questions. For example, to what extent does such behaviour impinge on personal and social interaction and on the individual psyche? Does it simply fill what were formerly extra or longer working hours with either discriminate or indiscriminate information gathering? Does it overload the brain with data, eventually causing confusion and a sort of dismayed inertia? Does it isolate us and exacerbate the despair and loneliness in people's lives? These are questions that have no easy answers and some people may dismiss them as fanciful. They are unlikely to be taken too seriously by the media itself, and if the media does not take them seriously then *who* will regard them as serious?

Unfortunately, much of the debate that occurs about the media is confined to journals that are widely unread and sometimes quite unreadable. Expecting the popular media to analyse itself in depth, and consistently, is expecting a lot, particularly when even the most responsible publications and channels are part of a pattern of media whose more significant impact transcends or subsumes its best elements. The structures and values of the media itself form part of the message received consciously or unconsciously by the public. These include an internal relationship of power between proprietor and employees and the adoption of consumerist or market criteria for gauging performance.

Even some independent academics are loathe to attach much significance to the possible serious effects of mass media consumption. They often, rightly, emphasise the resilience of the individual, the capacity of men, women and children to mediate any message by reference to other factors such as values that have been imbibed at home and in the school or factors such as the simple experience of daily life itself. People are right to reject knee-jerk, tabloid hysteria that immediately connects, for example, a particular act of violence with some current video or a controversial movie that may or may not have been seen by the perpetrator.

However, in their haste to eschew what they loosely term 'moral panics', academics and journalists may be slow to recognise the actual influence of media. It seems to me that this is so partly because, on the whole, they espouse liberal enlightenment values and fear that any admission that the media has effects on behaviour will strengthen the hand of conservative or reactionary elements in society. They dread being depicted, or even seeing themselves as a shining Knight of Columbanus or another Mary Whitehouse, whose campaigns about the quality of British TV were often derided in the last quarter of the twentieth century.

However, while there is no doubt that concerns about the possible effects of the media on individual behaviour can be exaggerated, it is also the case that liberal prejudices, vanity and complacency may prevent otherwise critical intellectuals and writers from perceiving qualitative and even quantum changes in the way media are conceived and delivered, changes that greatly enhance the possibility of media influencing human minds. Deregulation and increased competition, coupled with the sophisticated targeting of particular markets as well as the 'branding' of products, are creating a landscape in which, for many citizens, the media not only constitutes their culture but sets the agenda for what they regard as desirable, important or even realistic.

If academics and journalists have any doubts about the faith of the market in the media then they ought to look at the amount of money spent by the advertising industry.

In Ireland alone the figure for just above-the-line advertising is more than £450 million. That does not include fortunes spent on market research that predicts behaviour and tracks the results of campaigns. Anyone who thinks that such money is spent speculatively or that advertising executives doubt the influential power of media is deluding her or himself.

Moreover, it is not sufficient merely to look at the amount spent on advertising in Ireland to understand the impact of commercialism on the Irish media. To do so would be to omit considering the multiple ways in which global advertising and commercial promotion reinforce that impact. There are, for example, those TV channels that are beamed into Ireland carrying foreign advertisements. Then there are various video clips and other promotional material provided by commercial interests. This material gets into the media in a manner that it would not otherwise do if its provision were not free of charge. Such clips can even find their way onto supposedly independent factual programming without the public being aware that they have been provided by some third party.

Then there is the fact that very many extremely sophisticated and extraordinarily expensive advertisements are brought into Ireland already made, their costs entirely or largely recouped elsewhere. These may well be aesthetically attractive and are often amusing but they are also the result of intensive planning, which addresses people's psychology in order to trigger behavioural responses. They constitute a Pavlovian strategy, whose success is measured inch by inch in the careful monitoring of sales and results by advertisers.

Within the advertising industry itself there is no doubt that advertisements work. Every day of the week across the globe, fortunes and jobs depend on demonstrating clearly to clients that this is so. Some of the big TV studios in the United States even ape advertising industry techniques by deliberately constructing their popular series in a way that subconsciously stimulates viewing, including among other methods the rewriting of scripts in accordance with the advice of behavioural psychologists.

Any impact that such commercialisation has on the individual is further exacerbated by strategies that deliberately target people in an integrated fashion. One such strategy involves the creation by media organisations of niche audiences that can then be delivered to advertisers. Another strategy is to keep the citizen in her or his niche even when the television is turned off.

With the expansion of television and radio services it has become easier but also commercially essential to give people the stimuli that they want and expect from particular channels. Thus, some young people may always turn on, say, FM104 because they know that they will hear what they like and will never turn on Radio 1 because they regard it as 'boring'. Similarly, those who watch Network 2 may seldom watch BBC2. Within their particular cocoon or niche they can then be continually bombarded with the stimuli that market research shows tickle their demographic fancies. This keeps them watching the ads and in a mood to buy, or at least in a mood to associate the products advertised with feelings of pleasure. As these niches have become more clearly defined, the shared public space of radio and television has collapsed and viewers of one kind of channel are unlikely to know much about what viewers of another like or watch. This has particular implications for general public awareness about the content and style of channels aimed at children and young adults in their formative years.

One implication of this increased specialisation and heightened commercial sensitivity is that certain kinds of programmes may not be included in the schedules of some channels, or included only peripherally, because they spoil the party mood and interrupt the flow of commercial bonhomie. It is quite possible that if the media *does* influence behaviour, as advertisers certainly believe it does, then the mere absence of certain kinds of programming and of points of view or paradigms that challenge the dominant ethos may contribute to the atrophy of people's intellects and to the blunting of their political and social sensitivities. People lose the media vocabulary with which to articulate their needs constructively.

If the narrowness of niches is a cause for concern, then so too is the way in which the entertainment industry is moulding everyday experience, so that when we turn off the telly or the radio we are still massaged by the messages of consumerism as we enter public transport, do our shopping or go out for an evening's pleasure. The young person may move from their niche TV channel onto a bus, which itself is an advertisement. The unquestioned ease with which Dublin Bus and other companies have been able to impose a commercial shell on public transport users, even darkening windows to make the external message larger, is itself an indication of how dominant the consumer paradigm is in our society. Climbing on board such buses, or entering DART stations, which seem to be frequently rented out to single advertisers to paste with propaganda for alcohol or sugar-laden confectionery, the citizen may retreat from such gloom and ugliness to their Walkman, where they are likely to listen to a niche radio channel.

Even our shopping experience is becoming a privatised environment in which gated shopping centres are themselves themed and manipulated in the interests of big money. Inside the main shopping malls (and even public streets increasingly look like malls as they are bought up by shopping chains) people flock to brand-name shops for their sports gear or buy the music of bands targeted at their age group and cross-promoted heavily on the niche channels to which they are most likely to listen. Indeed, the pattern of their consumerism is itself reflected back into patterns of investment in the media, as evidenced by the recent round of applications for a licence to provide Dublin with a radio station aimed at younger people. Owners of existing radio stations joined forces with newspaper proprietors, music industry personnel, nightclub owners and others to attempt a horizontal integration of their activities.

While one does not wish to be too alarmist about what might be regarded as a trend towards 'Consumer Totalitarianism', it is disappointing but not remarkable that so little public debate takes place about its implications. The reason that it is *not* remarkable is firstly that this trend reflects the ideology of our wealthy consumerist society and secondly that media organisations that depend on advertising to survive are disinclined to interrogate it too harshly.

The trump card of what might be called dramatically (and possibly without undue exaggeration) 'Consumer Totalitarianism' is that its servants claim with considerable justification to be giving people what they want, as if indulging material attachments or fantasies was somehow a moral value or was, *per se,* socially desirable. At the same time, like the feeding of any habit, it is also stimulating greater attachment to and fantasies regarding consumerism.

One particular aspect of the media strategy of the entertainment industry that is particularly interesting, if not insidious, is the phenomenon of 'branding', whether it is the 'branding' of a whole channel or of a particular product. For example, new stations set out to create their own brand image, one that is consistent with the brands on which a particular service will depend for advertising. Commonly used to refer to the process of burning an identifying mark on cattle or prisoners, 'branding' has also come to be applied by advertisers to the process of creating an 'image' for products and services.

As boundaries between the image of the product and the self-image of the consumer blur, 'branding' recovers some of its primary meaning. Thus, people feel compelled to brand themselves as members of a transnational fashion cult by wearing the images and names of manufacturers such as, for example, Nike or Adidas or Calvin Klein. Young people may brand themselves partly as a means of hiding in the herd and attempting to escape vulnerable isolation. A highly sophisticated advertising and music industry, replete with the expertise of psychology and other knowledge, avidly encourages them to do so.

For its part, the media industry, in the course of 'targeting' and 'branding', spends big amounts on audience research and on pre-production, which includes, for example, the construction of restrictive 'play-lists' that ensure that radio programme presenters may never stray far from the immediate gratification of their listeners. In this hidden world of audience manipulation, even the number of 'beats-per-minute' is measured and deliberately or automatically factored into what is allowed to become part of a particular media environment.

Particular kinds of music elicit a definite response in listeners and that is where 'beats-per-minute' can be relevant: generally not too few for younger and not too many for older listeners. People want their buzz from their box and relevant information is increasingly provided in bite-size pieces that make one nostalgic for the 'three-minute culture'. Audiences use the media for a number of reasons and not all of these are intellectual or aesthetic. The 'rock 'n' roll' factor is significant, as people tune in deliberately to be excited or stimulated, to hear, see or get a 'hit'. Stimulation is crucial in the process of attracting audiences. The word 'hit', referring as it does to a popular music disc (as well as to taking drugs), is often used in this context. The word extends the metaphor of dominance or belligerent possession suggested by 'targeting' and 'branding'.

One of the prime functions of stimulation is the creation of an environment in which people are responsive to the sales messages of advertisers. There will be a 'go-getting', 'feel-good' aspect to a station's identity if it is to create the most receptive context for the branding exercises of corporate giants and others. Party poopers are definitely unwelcome in such a world. An aggressively 'positive' ideology, like that associated with the Celtic Tiger, sits very comfortably with the construction of an audience that is seen, and encouraged to see itself, as moving forward on a wave of material satisfaction and acquisition.

It is true to say that broadcasters try to satisfy the desires of their intended audiences and claim fairly to 'give people what they want', but the 'chicken-and-egg' question may legitimately be asked of broadcasting executives and shareholders. Which is the chicken? Is it the station that makes the audience or the audience that determines the station? It seems that each influences the other. Of course the audience is not entirely passive. It can tune out but it is, nevertheless, reactive and its reaction is carefully conditioned by media interests. Commercial pressures may result in the exclusion from schedules of expressions of the taste and preferences of those who have little disposable income or the exclusion of material that is not an instant commercial 'hit'.

In a very competitive media environment, station management will also be disinclined to bite the commercial hand that feeds it by challenging forcefully the interests or ideology of the dominant groups that provide investment and advertising. An audience may well be appreciative of hard-hitting investigative journalism or fierce social satire – and may in fact desire this – but not get it.

Thus, the media can be 'read' as indicators of social relationships, as well as creators of social reality. While the public embraces services planned on the basis of consumer spending patterns and research, such data is further considered by station managers in the light of the wishes and budgets of advertisers. In this way there is created a media product or 'brand' that is inclined to lull rather than challenge audiences when it comes to dominant cultural, economic and social values. Any 'shocks' provided are likely to be at the expense of those whose power does not extend to the commercial sphere. 'Daring' DJs and cynical stand-up comics may deride traditional values or help to erode local identity rather than mock consumerism or question globalisation.

The tendency towards a hermetic relationship between a station, its audience and advertisers is exacerbated by technical developments and policy changes. These have made it possible to franchise an increasing number of stations and, therefore, made it necessary to cater for particular 'niches' that are commercially viable because they 'deliver' very specific kinds of audiences to advertisers, in a cost-effective manner. One applicant for the Dublin youth franchise noted that, 'as the number of stations increases, so the market becomes more and more fragmented. Therefore, a defined niche market will be an advantage for any station'. Another proclaimed, 'Mass market targeting strategies will be replaced by more niche targeting. This will lead to reduced media wastage for advertisers and increased revenues to targeted media'. In such broadcasting contexts philosophical aspirations to a coherent 'public sphere' disintegrate in practice as private broadcasters – or 'narrow-casters' to be exact – capture and fragment the attention of the public right from the moment that infants first get hooked on cartoon channels that are programmed by multinationals and linked to merchandising strategies.

If what I am saying sounds somewhat Orwellian, I would ask you to bear in mind that I have been describing actual practices in the entertainment industry and have not engaged in futuristic predictions. I have also pointed to those behavioural responses that are closely and scientifically monitored by market research and that indicate clearly how the investment of large amounts of money in media does have an effect on human behaviour. Since this is so, it is fair to interrogate the consequences of such effects and to ask who is ensuring that those who control the media, use it in a manner that is not manipulative of the human mind and not unfair to those interests who do not have the kind of disposable income that the funders of modern media regard as their principle focus of interest. Where broadcasting was once seen as a means of informing, educating and entertaining, it is now seen increasingly as a way of entertaining and selling.

However, before turning then to some appropriate responses to the challenge of contemporary media, permit me please to make an affirmation: Television is a power for good. It can be inspiring and joyful; it is frequently informative and fun. Radio is a wonderful medium, intimate and educational, tuneful and dramatic. The newspapers are a source of valuable information, and journalists who work for them have helped to root out some of the dark secrets of Irish society and to liberate citizens from lies about our society and how it works. The Internet is a source of wonder and a possible means of uniting fragmented communities globally.

For these very reasons it is crucial that citizens take a more active interest in the matter of who controls the media, who monitors the media, what the media actually says or implies and how the media creates or reinforces peoples' opinions, identity and value systems. The gap between the media's own understanding of its role or power and the public's understanding of the media is considerable. In my opinion, even those who should know better (including many academics, journalists, community activists, educators and religious practitioners) either shy away from the reality of media because it is so powerful and complex, or deny the reality because they, like most citizens, refuse to accept the fact that we are all influenced by the media. The naive response, 'Oh it doesn't affect me', keeps advertising executives happy. Many educators and religious practitioners also feel that they have enough on their plates without having to analyse media issues, and such attention as they do pay tends to focus on particular incidents that are explicitly sexual or violent or that relate to hate speech.

Now I am not going to dwell here on the issue of sex and violence in the media. It is deeply depressing just how cheaply sexualised so much of the entertainment industry has become and it is at society's peril that one ignores the effect of this on teenagers. Such content boosts audiences, sells products and constitutes a pressure on adolescents to experiment with sex at an early age. Realities such as unwanted pregnancies, abortion, AIDS and hearts broken for life are seldom part of the picture.

There is also something very disturbing about the obscenity of violence that sees factual and fictional programmes attempt to outdo one another in graphic imagery and brutal detail in order to hold the attention of viewers.

The pushing of alcohol in the media has also become a problem. Expensive billboard campaigns and costly cross-promotions between advertising, sponsorship and entertainment events deliberately play with adolescent self-identity and even encourage deviousness or facetiousness about liquor consumption. How clear are the consciences of advertisers about their strategies?

Ambiguous, self-interested messages are embedded in commercial contexts that generally subvert criticism by representing it as fuddy-duddy and boringly inevitable, or that misrepresent infantile rebelliousness and recklessness as radical action and freedom. We have a major substance abuse problem in Ireland, which includes alcohol as well as drugs, but you'd never guess from the ads that the abuse of alcohol causes so much misery. I believe that the laws on the promotion and sale of alcohol need to be tightened up to protect adolescents against exploitation, and I do not regard the present self-regulation by the industry as adequate. In particular, I believe that billboard advertising for spirits should be banned and that broadcasters ought to be prevented by European Law from broadcasting any event sponsored by drink labels, especially as these sponsored events convey the impression that the relationship between alcohol and recreation is not problematic.

I acknowledge that Irish broadcasters do not advertise spirits above 25% proof and that RTE carries no alcohol advertising on 2FM. These restrictions present particular difficulties because UK stations such as Channel 4 and Ulster Television do in fact advertise spirits and are freely received in the Republic of Ireland where they compete with RTE and TV3 for advertising revenue. In relation specifically to RTE's self-imposed ban on alcohol ads on 2FM, it must also be noted that competing IRTC stations are not similarly restrained. Such anomalies point to the urgent necessity for closer co-ordination of broadcasting regulations at a national and European level, so that those stations that are most responsible about alcohol suffer no commercial disadvantage.

Moreover, the alcohol companies are cunning when it comes to circumventing regulations. Trade names such as Smirnoff or Bacardi are attached to low alcohol drinks that can be advertised within existing restrictions, thus in effect giving the better known and harder drinks associated with those names a free ride. Then there is the use of trade names in connection with big sporting events, which can scarcely be ignored. There is the massive use of media such as bill-boards to mount very visual and directed campaigns that logically should be restricted when radio and television advertisements for alcohol are restricted.

The alcohol industry may claim that it is impossible to prove a direct causal relationship between ads and alcohol abuse but in pushing alcohol they increase the likelihood of abuse. They also create an atmosphere of tolerance and even an attitude of amusement around alcohol as a way of life. One current campaign actually encourages surreptitious drinking while many others constitute a form of propaganda that circumvents specific regulations to cast alcohol in an attractive light as something socially enhancing. It is way past time for the rest of society to take alcohol advertising as seriously as the alcohol industry itself does.

However, although there is much to be discussed about the way in which the media and entertainment industries have successfully exploited adolescence in an ever more sophisticated fashion, I want to avoid getting bogged down in particular examples. Furthermore, while educating people in the realities of media production and in the analysis of particular media content is both necessary and useful, what is required urgently is a much broader critique of the media. This will alert people to the fact that embedded in our consumer culture is a surrogate system of faith and civic values that may be helping to change our concepts of society and the self, and may also be retarding the exploration or development of historical and spiritual insights, which are instinctively sensed by media promoters to stand in the way of consumerism and global capitalism.

Yet, even as I call for a more sophisticated approach by educators and religious practitioners to understanding media, I am conscious of the fact that commercialism is already seeping into classrooms and that this is no accident. Schools have been targeted deliberately by some commercial strategists and, in any event, the Internet acts as a carrier for commercials. In some countries there is even evidence of the commercialisation through sponsorship of religious gatherings or places.

For their part, religious practitioners have, I believe, great power to provide a counterpoint to what I have only half-jokingly calling 'Consumer Totalitarianism'. However, I believe that the largest Irish Christian church, as currently organised, stands especially in need of institutional reform and I am certainly not suggesting that much can be achieved by hierarchical edicts. What I am optimistic about are the challenges that can be provided by, firstly, actual examples of lifestyles that challenge the crazed competitiveness and consumerism of modern western society and, secondly, the example of that meditative stillness, which a small but growing number of practitioners are coming to realise has a creative power.

Elected and creative meditative silence provides a truly fundamental challenge to the constant babble and chatter of the media and to the entertainment environment in which we are immersed. Lived example and meditative awareness can be greatly enhanced by the encouragement of dialogue about the relationship between society, religion and culture. A small experiment in such dialogue took place at Dublin City University earlier this year, involving students, academics, journalists and the representatives of various faiths. It proved to be highly exciting and, in the opinion of most students, very successful. If the churches wish to empower lay people to play a greater role in challenging the value systems embedded in media and entertainment messages, then they could change their own power structures and create mechanisms for lay participation that are broadly based and include not only the most orthodox thinkers.

However, it cannot be left up to ordinary citizens individually or even in small groups to cope with the influence and power of what is now a global entertainment and media industry. Governments and regulators must do more. A naive 'light touch' approach to regulation is a disservice to the public when media strategies themselves are so highly planned and resourced. Moreover, any regulation, if it is to be effective today, must be co-ordinated internationally and such intervention should involve commercial interests being compelled to meet certain obligations and not simply entail the expenditure of public monies on minority programming. The European Union can and does play a central role in improving the media and making it more accountable. It is vitally important that our government ministers, regardless of their particular understanding of the role and vision of the European Union, play as full a part as possible in EU meetings that relate to cultural matters.

In Ireland we need greater public investment in the forward planning and analysis of media trends and content. Already much of the Irish media is foreign-owned and more of it could be sold off any day now. RTÉ is in a state of financial and philosophical crisis. TnaG, or TG4 if you like, is another symbol of that lip service that has been paid to the Irish language since the foundation of the State. There continues to be an absence of clear political thinking and of the system of funding to make such cultural initiatives effective. Within the context of the European Union, small countries such as Ireland have special reasons to be at the forefront in fostering debate about the control and content of the media.

Finally, and more specifically, the citizens of Ireland deserve a new mechanism for dealing effectively with complaints about the media. For that reason I am advocating the establishment of a self-regulatory Press Complaints Commission. Already the Broadcasting Complaints Commission provides a limited means of responding to unfair treatment by a radio or TV service, although Ireland appears to be in default of its obligations under the European Directive known as 'Television Without Frontiers' because of its failure to provide to citizens a right-of-reply on the airwaves. Even where the Broadcasting Complaints Commission finds in your favour, it has no power to require a broadcaster to report that decision, let alone afford the aggrieved party a right-of-reply. Successive Broadcasting Complaints Commissions are appointed every five years by the government of the day.

In relation to the print media, Ireland lacks any form of press council or press complaints commission such as exists in other jurisdictions including the United Kingdom, Australia and Canada. This absence is due partly to the failure of successive governments to implement the findings of the Commission on the Newspaper Industry 1996. For a press council to work effectively, our draconian libel laws need to be reformed (they need to be reformed anyway to put an end to the excessive and oppressive intervention by lawyers that is inhibiting free reporting). This is not for a moment to suggest that such a complaints commission would replace reasonable libel laws; rather it would enhance them. In my opinion the newspapers themselves could immediately establish an interim press council. They may be reluctant to do so because of a suspicion that this would ease pressure on the government to reform the current libel laws, which some politicians are slow to remove because they fear further investigation.

Any complaints commission that is appointed ought to be self-regulatory but robust and, like that of the United Kingdom, be chaired and composed mainly of people who have no direct connection to the media industry. While self-regulation has its limits, it is preferable to government regulation, which at times of crisis could become distinctly sinister. Indeed there may be a good argument ultimately for dismantling the present Broadcasting Complaints Commission and creating an all-encompassing self-regulatory body, perhaps with two distinct subcommittees, one for the print and one for the electronic media. While Broadcasting Complaints Commissions have worked fairly and reasonably since their inceptions, there is nothing to prevent a particular government from appointing a group of people to it who do not reflect the broad consensus of society and who could become a serious inhibition on freedom of speech, notwithstanding the ultimate safeguard of the Constitution of Ireland.

So what I am suggesting is the possibility of a self-regulatory Complaints Commission appointed by the media, which will draw up a code of practice or standards for the industry as a whole, or at least for the press. These standards should cover such matters as:

- Accuracy
- Privacy
- Harassment
- Intrusion into grief or shock
- Children
- Sex, rape and marital cases
- Victims
- Depiction of violence and death
- Behaviour of the media in hospitals and cemeteries
- Reporting of crime
- Misrepresentation
- Disclosure of relevant facts
- Discrimination on the grounds of race, disability, etc.
- Listening devices and hidden cameras
- Confidential sources
- Payment for articles

The purpose of a code of standards is not to inhibit freedom of speech or to impose any kind of political correctness, but to create through self-regulation an environment in which the public may have confidence that individual citizens are likely to be treated fairly or to have some comeback if they are not; and also to enhance the reputation of journalists who generally enjoy, as frequent opinion polls indeed show, the confidence and esteem of the public.

As I have already indicated, such a Complaints Commission is just one of the building blocks in any new media strategy. The strategy should also involve greater commitment by both the government and regulators to creating a democratic and moral media environment and should see an enhanced role for educators and religious practitioners. That role would include fostering a far more sophisticated awareness among the public of the wide range and depth of issues involved in understanding the role that the media and entertainment industries play in shaping our lives and thoughts.

When I first saw the programme for this conference and read the titles of many of the papers, I immediately thought 'Media'. When Professor Gearóid Ó Tuathaigh considers 'relationships of power', when Maureen Gaffney talks of 'the ethic of care in Irish society' or when Kathleen Lynch addresses 'social justice and equality', who can ignore the fact that the media is ultimately 'top down' when setting its agendas (no matter how much market research will purport to pander to what people want)?

Who can ignore the fact that 'the ethic of care' has too few beats-per-minute to survive in the jangled world of many contemporary TV and radio schedules or that the concept of social equality contradicts the adoration of disposable income by media financiers and advertisers?

When Professor Robert Lane speaks of 'putting people at the centre of things' who could ignore the fact that in most living rooms the centre of things is the television set and that the role of public ownership or policy in television is shrinking while that of unaccountable, multinational, media conglomorates and entertainment millionaires advances in leaps, bounds and billions?

When Fr Seán McDonagh asks 'Why are we deaf to the cry of the earth?' the answer lies partly in the fact that we can no longer hear the voice of the poor or see the world of nature beyond the clutter of commercial schedules and the comfort of our media blanket.

Redefining the role of media and of our relationship to it is a task both for the government and for the individual. The fact that the task is so daunting and that the forces of consumerism are so great should not deter us from asserting our freedom from manipulation.

VIEW FROM THE CHAIR

David McWilliams

There's nothing better than a feeling of insecurity to ease you into a job. Why not get an economist to chair a session entitled, 'Economics, As If People Mattered?' Great craic Harry; with friends like you, who needs enemies?

Now I know just how low us purveyors of the dismal science have sunk in recent years. But why? Is not the economy booming? Are we not all rich beyond our recent dreams? Yet something appears to be missing. Economics never suggested that it had all the answers, but this session reminded me just how removed we are, at times, from the questions.

It's a quarter to ten, the hall is packed and the punters are restless. Clink, clink, the sound of metal on glass, order, order, gulp of water, quick intro and off we go. Orla Kelly, first up and with the almost impossible task of persuading a sceptical audience that large multi-nationals care. 'Managing diversity' – what a perfect term for a changing workforce. But is it just a workforce? Orla's answer was a resounding no. In fact, she continued, the Hewlett Packard experience in the US indicated that diversity is strength. Orla stressed that the organisation must adapt to the workforce, not vice versa. The crowd applauded, keeping their powder dry.

Up stepped local man, John Liddy, to bolster the 'people matter to corporations' line. And a fine job he did too. Roche, the Swiss pharmaceutical giant, has been a presence in Clare for many years and, although the hall appeared to have its fair share of doubters, John's comprehensive insight into corporate thinking at Roche – from their Schools' Link Project to their Employee Development Programme – pointed to a company with its eye on the ball.

The punters were satisfied. Questions, sometimes thinly disguised statements, slammed in, blaming multi-nationals for all sorts of misdeeds. Our speakers parried well, observing that with the local economy booming, workers could and would vote with their feet. Some in the crowd remained uneasy. Time out. Coffee.

Twelve noon, up stepped a man of great dignity, wisdom and generosity. Professor Robert Lane, who had travelled from the States with his charming wife Helen, took the stage. It's very simple – people, relationships and family. Money only has value when you don't have it. When a country gets enough of it, it loses its allure. Ireland, he contended, is in that phase where money is no longer delivering. The US reached that stage twenty or thirty years ago. As the wise Professor put it, 'it ain't worth it anymore'. Now this wasn't some off the cuff remark, rather it was based on years and years of painstaking research. Survey after survey pointed out that rich people are no happier than are those on average incomes and, in many cases, they become less happy or less satisfied the richer they become. Possessions, status, brands, cars, watches, big houses and such stand for nowt. The old man struck a chord. The crowd loved him. Some might argue he was preaching to the converted. That may be so, but it was poignant, fascinating and thoughtful stuff. Spot on. A burst of applause, followed by another and another.

'Don't worry', Fr Seán McDonagh said to me as I asked about his background, 'I'm just a missionary who is into flowers.' Flowers, how are you? What followed can only be described as a passionate, invigorating tour de force, hammering home the message of wanton environmental destruction. Then McDonagh changed tack, focussing on the destruction of Clare, the Burren and the local fishing village of Kilkee. You could hear a pin drop. In a coherently argued, ten-minute burst, Seán used slides, photos, local records and documents to describe how greed and stupidity were ruining one of Ireland's most beautiful places. We were captivated. Will I be lynched for calling time? Yes, but the floor was buzzing and questions were guaranteed. Sean's message was straightforward: greed is ruining our planet and if we don't have the environment, then we have nothing. The government is not only irresponsible but, in the pocket of developers, acting cowardly as it turns the proverbial blind eye. As we 'fumbled in the greasy till', our precious country was being sacrificed for the price of a '00 D' BMW.

'How do you follow that?' I asked our final speaker. With calm authority, Colum Kenny answered. Kenny told it as it is. The media services, not politicians, are the new power, and advertising, branding, consumerism and manipulation are its stock in trade. We are watching more TV, absorbing more ideas, acting as sponges for a diet of marketing cliches and consumerist dreams. Widespread alcohol advertising, for example, elevates to glamour status one of our single biggest social ills and yet we're not batting an eyelid. The Internet is another conduit for media manipulation and, without powerful central control and monitoring, the media will very soon usurp politics as the key opinion maker in our society. Not for the fainthearted, yet delivered with the clarity of a mind that can see way into the future. Excellent stuff.

On that note, the Chairman – a man who earns his crust from economics and the commercial media – thought it best to round up procedures. The fact that we were way overtime and many questions had to be left for the bar, underscored what a brilliant, refreshing day we had all experienced.

CONTRIBUTORS

William (Bill) Paul Collins is presently Associate Professor in the History/Political Science Department at Samford University, Alabama. He was Visiting Professor at the University of Alabama from 1985–87, Associate Professor at Drake University from 1979–86, and Assistant Professor at Georgia State University from 1973–79.

Awards include Teacher of the Year, Samford University 1991; Teacher of the Year, Drake University, 1983; NEH Summer Fellow, University of Iowa, 1984.

He is the author of many publications, including *An Ecological Theory of Democracy: Steps Toward a Non-Equilibruim View of Politics* and *Does Democracy Inevitably Imply Hierarchy?*

His current work is a translation of Aquinas's Commentary on Aristotle's politics. This supports his concern with the origins and foundation of modern political philosophy.

Maureen Gaffney is a well-known psychologist, broadcaster and writer. Since 1993 she has been Chairperson of the National Economic and Social Forum (NESF), which was set up by the government to advise on policies in relation to unemployment, poverty and social exclusion. The Forum includes representatives of all the political parties, local and central government, the trade unions, businesses, farming organisations as well as the voluntary and community sector. She was a Law Reform Commissioner from 1986–1996, and Senior Lecturer and Director of the Doctoral Programme in Clinical Psychology in Trinity College, Dublin, for many years.

She is a member of the Council of the Economic and Social Research Institute (ESRI) and also a member of the Insurance Ombudsman Council. Dr Gaffney also works as a consultant on issues relating to human resources, leadership and the management of change. She was born in Middleton, County Cork, and was educated at University College, Cork, the University of Chicago, and Trinity College, Dublin.

Colum Kenny is a Senior Lecturer in Communications at Dublin City University. A barrister and author of books on Irish history, he writes regularly about media matters for the *Sunday Independent* and other publications. In 1998 he was appointed a member of the Independent Radio and Television Commission.

Robert E. Lane is Eugene Meyer Professor Emeritus of Political Science at Yale University. Prof. Lane received a BS from Harvard College in 1939, as well as a PhD in Political Economy and Government in 1950. He has been President of the American Political Science Association, the Policy Studies Organisation and the International Society of Political Psychology. He has been Fellow of the Centre for Advanced Study in the Behavioural Sciences, Fellow of the Netherlands Institute for Advanced Study and Fellow of the British Academy as well as Senior Fulbright-Hayes Research Scholar (UK).

As well as being a prolific contributor of articles and book chapters, his own publications include *Political Ideology: Why the American Common Man Believes What He Does, The Market Experience,* and *The Loss of Happiness in Market Democracies.* His most recent publication is *Diminishing Returns to Income, Companionship – Happiness.*

He has long been regarded as one of the foremost thinkers in the field of behavioural sciences and argues that the main sources of well-being in advanced economies are friendships and a good family life.

Kathleen Lynch is a founder member and co-ordinator of the Equality Studies Centre at University College, Dublin. She has a deep and longstanding commitment to the understanding and promotion of equality and social justice both locally and globally. To achieve this objective, Professor Lynch believes it is necessary to promote the democratisation of knowledge and understanding, so that all people in society can benefit from the research being produced in universities and other institutes of learning.

Professor Lynch has published widely on issues of equality and is currently working on a book with her colleagues in UCD on Equality: Theory and Practice. Her most recent book, *Equality in Education* (1999), is published by Gill and Macmillan. She is also the author of *The Hidden Curriculum* (1989) and co-author of *Schools and Society in*

Ireland (1993). She has co-edited two major studies in sociology, *Ireland: A Sociological Profile* (1986) and *Irish Society: Sociological Perspectives* (1995).

Seán McDonagh grew up in County Tipperary, close to the shores of Lough Derg, He was ordained a priest in 1969. The next three years were spent in parish and teaching ministry in the Philippines as a Columbian missionary.

After graduate studies in anthropology and linguisitics at Catholic University and Georgetown University, Washington, DC (1972–75), he taught anthropology and served as chaplain at Mindanao State University. While there he became involved in Christian-Muslim dialogue and in local environmental issues, especially tropical deforestation. When he worked among the T'boli people of South Cotabato (1980 onwards) his concern for the destruction of the environment grew.

He is the author of three books – *To Care for the Earth, The Greening of the Church* and *Passion for the Earth* – as well as numerous articles in magazines in Ireland, Britian, the US, Australia and the Philippines.

Seán is co-ordinator of the Justice, Peace and Integrity of Creation Programme of the Columban Missionary Society worldwide, as well as Chair of the Irish environmental organisation VOICE.

David McWilliams
David McWilliams was educated at Trinity College, Dublin, and the College of Europe in Bruges. In 1993, after four years working as an economist in the Central Bank of Ireland, he became the youngest-ever director at Union Bank of Switzerland, with responsibility for the bank's global investment strategy. He was the first economist to accurately predict a non-inflationary boom that later became known as the Celtic Tiger.

In 1997, David moved to the Banque Nationale de Paris where he was Chief Economist and Head of Research, specialising in Russia, Eastern Europe and Latin America. David returned to Dublin last year and now works for a New York based investment boutique. He also presents TV3's flagship current affairs programme *Agenda* and writes a regular economics and finance column for the Sunday Business Post.

Mick O'Connell

A native of Valentia Island, County Kerry, Mick O'Connell is regarded by many as the greatest Gaelic footballer of all time. *A Kerry Footballer* (Mercier Press, 1974) is an autobiographical account of his rise to stardom. He has been described as a true free spirit and a man of great sincerity. Brendan Kennelly says of him, 'The island clay felt good beneath his feet; a man undeceived by victory or defeat.' A promising engineering student and a national figure, following his exploits on the playing field, the door was open to Mick to have chosen any one of several high-profile careers. Instead he decided his future lay on Valentia, in pursuit of the island traditions of fishing and farming. Mick is married to Rosaleen, a native of Cavan, and they have three children, Díarmuid, Máire and Mícheál.

Kate Ó Dubhchair

Kate Ó Dubhchair is Senior Lecturer in Informatics at the University of Ulster and Professor of Community Informatics in the Graduate School of Public Policy in the University of Missouri. Kate has twenty years' experience of working and researching the use of information communication technologies in the community. She has to her credit over thirty publications. Her current interests include community in the knowledge society and the ethical implications of the information age. She is a founder member of Fermanagh University Partnership Board. This unique model of education involves Community and University in partnership for life-long learning and economic development. She is the President of the European Rural University, a Pan-European learning community and also a Research Fellow of the United States Rural Policy Research Institute (RUPRI).

Gearóid Ó Tuathaigh is Associate Professor of History at the National University of Ireland, Galway. He was a former Dean of Arts and Vice-President of NUI, Galway. He was educated at University College, Galway, and at Peterhouse, Cambridge. He has been a Visiting Professor at the University of Toronto and has lectured at numerous universities throughout the US, Australia, the UK and continental Europe. He has published widely – in Irish and English – on modern Irish and British history, mainly of the nineteenth and twentieth century. He is a Fellow of the Royal Historical Society, a Member of the Senate of the National University of Ireland, a former Member of the Ireland/USA Fulbright Commission and Cathaoirleach of Údarás na Gaeltachta during the period 1996–1999.

CONFERENCE 2001

IS THE FUTURE MY RESPONSIBILITY?

Examining Radical Change, Institutional Relevance, and Individual Responsibility

CONFERENCE '98 posed the question 'Are We Forgetting Something?' and dealt with the need to achieve a balance between a caring society and a consumer-oriented society in this era of the Celtic Tiger.

CONFERENCE '99, 'Working Towards Balance', continued the debate by trying to recognise the human dimension of the workplace in this increasingly career and work-oriented society.

CONFERENCE 2000 brought this one step further in the personal realm by addressing the topic 'Redefining Roles and Relationships'.

CONFERENCE 2001
Conference Centre, West County Hotel,
Ennis, County Clare
7 – 9 November 2001

For further information please contact:
Máire Johnston, Conference Co-ordinator
Rural Resource Development Ltd
Town Hall, Shannon, Co Clare
Tel 061 361 144 • Fax 061 361 954
Email rrd@eircom.net or millcon.ennis@eircom.net